The Complete Book of
HERBS & SPICES

D1286235

Growing, Harvesting, and Preparing Herbs
for Cooking, Lotions, and Home-Remedies

The Complete Book of
HERBS & SPICES

Brenda Little

Boca Raton Public Library, Boca Raton, FL

Silverleaf Press Books are available exclusively
through Independent Publishers Group.

For details write or telephone
Independent Publishers Group, 814 North Franklin St.
Chicago, IL 60610, (312) 337-0747

Silverleaf Press
8160 South Highland Drive
Sandy, Utah 84093

Copyright © 2006 by Silverleaf Press
All rights reserved. This book, or parts thereof, may
not be produced in any form without permission.
ISBN 1-933317-51-5

Contents

Introduction

No one book can possibly encompass all there is to know about herbs and spices. Man has been learning about the plants that share his environment from his earliest days and though the accumulated knowledge is now encyclopaedic, it is still very sketchy. It is estimated that there are at least half a million species of plant in the world, but only about 10 percent of the organic constituents have been identified. Linnaeus said: "What we know of the Divine works are much fewer than those of which we are ignorant" and his words are as true today as they were 200 years ago.

Knowledge has always come slowly. For primitive man the ability to make use of wild plants was a long, difficult process of trial and error—death must frequently have been the result of experimentation; the sun, the moon and the weather were his only teachers, personal observation was his only tool. During the millennia in which the hunter became the agriculturist and the nomadic way of life gave way to permanent settlement, plans became more recognized as providers of both food and medicine so that by the time the early civilizations had learned how to retain information by the inscription of character on tablets of papyri, they could list almost a thousand plants which were useful to man.

The Arab medical schools of the 9th century, the Greeks and Romans, the European botanists of the Renaissance all refined and expanded understanding of the properties contained in the "green healers" and this knowledge could be added to that of the great Chinese and Indian cultures. It is seldom sufficiently realized that until the early days of the present century, when the powerful petroleum and chemical industries began their dominance of our way of life, the plant was medicine as well as food to most of the world.

Synthetic drugs have largely ousted the natural medicines as the popular healers, but will these drugs be in use a thousand years from now, one wonders. Thyme will still be a powerful antiseptic and plantain leaves will still heal wounds, herbal medicines will still not cause the iatrogenic illnesses suffered by patients treated by synthetic drugs. We will doubtless never reach the stage where the medical needs of the world can be met by the use of medicinal plants alone and it would be foolish to negate all modern medicine, but our daily health and well-being can be greatly increased by knowledge of how the plants grown by our forefathers can still help us.

Growing them is simple and enjoyable; their use is simple. This simplicity should never be thought of as "simple" for it has the enduring quality of all great truths. Man is totally dependent on nature, no matter how clever he may be, and nature is bountiful. A new recognition both of that dependence and bounty is growing in the general public and science is showing a new interest in medical botany. It may be that in the years to come, ignorance of "Divine works" will be reduced at a speed which Linnaeus would never have dreamed possible.

Herb or spice?

The terms have come to be loosely used. For the purpose of this book the herb is taken to be a plant which does not develop woody tissue although there are exceptions such as Slippery Elm, a tree famous for the use of its bark, and Eucalyptus, etc.

An herb can be used whole or in part. Leaves, stems, flowers, seeds and roots can all have their uses as medicine, food, or a supplier of fragrance; it can be used fresh or dried. Herbs grow wild but can also be cultivated.

Spice is always the dried part of a plant and the main use is as a flavoring for food, although the medicinal properties are often present too. Spices come mainly from plants that grow in the hotter areas of the world and are cultivated for the "trade."

About Herbs and Spices

Plants classified as herbs produce in flower, root, leaf, stem or seed aromatic oils and man has learned to use them for culinary, medicinal, cosmetic and household purposes. All parts of the plant can be used fresh or dried.

Useful wild herbs are found all over the world and because they can be dried, their use is not confined to their indigenous environment, much as the leaves of tea—a native of the East, and can be used all over the world.

The gardener can use his native, cultivated herbs fresh or dried, or simply grow them for pleasure given by their color or fragrance. The early herb gardens were "physic gardens," regular in design to enable space to be conserved and cultivation kept easy but, as travelers brought home exotic plants which could be naturalized and gardening became not only utilitarian but an aesthetic joy, design became less formal. Today we find few "herb gardens" as such, the herb has taken a place among our flowers and vegetables and, to a large extent, its use has narrowed to culinary and salad purposes.

The choice of the herbs we grow in our gardens is a matter of individual interest and individual need; no firm lines can be laid down, but growing herbs have specific needs and there are certain basic rules to be followed if we are to make the best of their fragrance, color and remarkable properties.

Herbs and spices cultivation

Most herbs and spices need sun, a few need shade but all need a well-drained soil that is light and not over-rich. A good rule-of-thumb as to an herb's individual sun tolerance is supplied by its leaves; narrow, tough ones will happily take full sun, more tender ones prefer partial shade.

While the soil should not be rich it should certainly not be poor; mineral and organic content is as important to the herb as to any other plant. A light loam given a yearly application of organic compost is ideal. Herbs will not grow well in a heavy clayey soil that puddles after rain. Chemical fertilizers are likely to cause lush, extravagant growth and early collapse.

Herbs can be grown indoors and outdoors, in gardens, town backyards, balcony pots or window boxes, but their soil requirements remain constant. Look after the soil and your herbs will look after you.

Part II

Dictionary of the most widely used herbs and spices–their curative properties, use in the home, the garden, in cooking, and as cosmetic aids.

ACONITE — Monkshood, Wolfsbane, Blue Rocket, Helmet Flower

Botanical name: *Aconitum napellus*
Family: *Ranunculaceae*
Parts used: Roots and leaves
Poisonous herb

This tall perennial plant with spikes of helmet-shaped violet-blue flowers and serrated leaves, lighter green on the underside, is a European native that grows well in moist shady places in all temperate parts of the world.

The stems are smooth and round, the root is black and the seeds small, wrinkly and sharp-cornered. The plant can be propagated from seed or by division.

MEDICINAL USE: Sedative, febrifuge.

Although a poisonous plant, aconite has long been used in the treatment of fevers and inflammatory conditions, but home use is not recommended as there is no known reliable antidote for the poison. Used under medical supervision preparations made commercially can ease neuralgic and rheumatic pain and the feverish conditions associated with croup, tonsillitis and acute catarrh. It is also a heart sedative.

IN THE GARDEN

If you decide to include the plant for its beauty keep it in semi-shade and, if you must handle it, wear gloves.

AGRIMONY — Stickwort, Cocklebur, Church Steeples

Botanical name: *Agrimonia eupatoria*
Family: *Rosaceae*
Parts used: Roots and leaves

Agrimony grows wild in waste places and hedgerows in many temperate to warm areas of the world and some species have found their way into cultivation. It rarely grows more than about 35 inches (90cm) high and its appearance gives no clue that it belongs to the same family as the rose. The stem and narrow-toothed gray-green leaves are hairy and sticky to touch, the spikes of small yellow flowers open in sequence from the bottom of the slender stalks, and the seedpod, which carries only two seeds, is bristly—hence the name "Cocklebur."

MEDICINAL USE: Astringent, de-obstruent, diuretic, tonic.

A tea made from the leaves is good for bathing ulcerated varicose veins and persistent sores—an early botanist recommended it for wounds that became putrid after "fightings."

Since the plant is rich in iron, silica and Vitamins B and K, the tea also makes a good tonic drink and is not unpleasant when sweetened with honey. It will also relieve diarrhea and ease a cough. Local application will help to reduce excessive earwax.

COSMETIC USE

The tea, used as a face wash, is good for an open-pored oily skin.

Herbs and spices to grow

Though there are so many from which to choose—and we use far fewer today than did our grandparents—the old faithfuls continue to hold their place.

CULINARY HERBS GROWN FOR THEIR LEAVES

Angelica (perennial)
Balm (perennial)
Basil (annual)
Bay (perennial)
Borage (annual)
Burnet (biennial)
Chervil (biennial)
Chives (perennial)
Garlic (perennial)
Lovage (perennial)
Marjoram (perennial)
Mint (perennial)
Parsley (biennial)
Rosemary (perennial)
Sage (perennial)
Tarragon (perennial)
Thyme (perennial)

CULINARY HERBS AND SPICES GROWN FOR THEIR SEEDS

Anise (annual)
Caraway (biennial)

ALFAFA—Lucerne

Botanical name: *Medicago sativa*
Part used: Leaves

Best known as a crop grown for animal fodder,
Lucerne has a valuable place in the medicinal herbal.
The strong roots penetrate the soil so deeply they tap trace
minerals otherwise inaccessible and so make the plant a rich
source of iron, magnesium, phosphorus, potassium, sulfur, silicon
and Vitamin K.

CULINARY USE

Alfalfa seeds can be bought sprouted for use in salads and other food but it is
very simple to sprout one's own. Some people make quite a production of sprouting
seed but the following rough-and-ready fashion gives perfectly good results.

Place seeds in a jar, cover with water, then cover the jar with a piece of fine cloth and
leave overnight in a warm place. In the morning, tip the seeds into a colander and drain.
Replace them in the jar, re-cover with water and re-cover the jar. Do this every morning till the
seeds have sprouted to the length required.

SUMMER SOUP

A quick, simple and nourishing cold soup can be made by blending cut-
up tomatoes, green pepper, cucumber, celery and some chopped onion with
a good handful of alfalfa sprouts in tomato juice. The amounts can be varied
to individual taste. Blend until smooth and keep in the refrigerator until
ready to serve.

A version designed more for a party is made by blending tomato, pepper
and cucumber with a clove or two of garlic and then adding half a cup of
French dressing and a pinch of either dried coriander, cumin, anise (or even caraway seeds,
depending on individual taste) and then some finely chopped alfalfa sprouts and some chives,
again finely chopped. Put the mixture in the refrigerator until serving time, then add chilled

white wine and some iced water to bring it to soup consistency.

Both soups can be served with *croutons* of toast or with *croutons* of bread that have been spread with garlic butter and then baked in the oven until brown and crisp. Add alfalfa sprouts to a mixed salad or to an *omelette au fines herbes*. Always chop the sprouts well.

An enterprising cook can add food value to many dishes by the addition of the sprouted alfalfa. The taste is not strong and the presence will go undetected if the chopping is neat.

MEDICINAL USE: Tonic, de-toxicant.

Tea made from the leaves is a valuable tonic that athletes drink for added stamina, and nursing mothers to enrich and sustain their supply of breast milk.

It is also useful in the treatment of diabetes, rheumatism, jaundice, kidney complaints and anemia. Its detoxifying effect will help to cleanse the body of the accumulated poisons left after the use of synthetic drugs.

ALLSPICE — Pimento, Clove Pepper

Botanical name: *Pimento officinalis*
Family: *Myrtaceae*
Part used: Seed

When cooks buy allspice they are not, as is frequently thought, buying a mixture of spices, but the dried berry of one evergreen tree native to Central and South America and

Coriander (annual)
Dill (annual)
Fennel (biennial)

CULINARY HERBS GROWN FOR THEIR ROOTS

Horseradish (perennial)

Many herbs can be used for more than one purpose and some of the culinary ones can be used externally as an aid to beauty.

COSMETIC HERBS

Balm (perennial)
Bergamot (perennial)
Borage (annual)
Burdock (biennial)
Burnet (perennial)
Calendula (perennial)
Chamomile (perennial)
Chervil (biennial)
Comfrey (perennial)
Dandelion (perennial)
Fennel (biennial)
Lovage (perennial)
Mint (perennial)
Nasturtium (annual)
Nettle (perennial)
Parsley (perennial)
Rosemary (perennial)
Thyme (perennial)

the West Indies. The tree grows from 80-130 feet (25-40m) high and its small white flowers are followed by small rough fruits containing 2 kidney-shaped seeds. The fruits are gathered unripe and dried in the sun until they become a rich reddish-brown.

The tree is seldom cultivated out of its natural habitat as it will only grow under tropical conditions and few heated greenhouses would be large enough to house it.

CULINARY USE

The ground spice is used to flavor fish, meat, vegetables, cakes, puddings, soups, fruit pies, pickling spice and curry powder.

MEDICINAL USE: Stomachic, carminative.

The volatile oil obtained from the seed is used in medicines for stomach complaints and in preparations for the relief of toothache and headache.

ALOE
Family: *Liliaceae*
Part used: Leaves

Aloes are plants with large, green, thick, tapering leaves that grow in rosette form; when the leaves are snapped they exude a thick gel. A. *vera*, A. *ferox* and A. *socratina* are best known.

Aloes grow outdoors in the tropics where they put up a flower—usually red—with a tubular perianth, and can be grown indoors in more temperate climates.

They need very little water but must have a well-drained soil and protection from both scorching sun and sharp cold. Propagation can be made by pulling off a basal shoot and planting it.

MEDICINAL USE: Laxative, anthelmintic, balsamic.

A dried preparation of the gel is used for constipation and the expulsion of threadworms—it should not be used by pregnant women.

The gel, used fresh, is excellent for the relief of burns and abrasions—just snap off a leaf and apply the cut edge to the wound. A pot of aloe kept on the kitchen windowsill makes a splendid first-aid plant when clumsy handling of a hot iron or oven shelf has caused painful burning. Medical studies have provided evidence that sufferers from both ulcers and arthritis can be helped by internal dosage.

COSMETIC USE

The dried skin of eczema will respond to frequent applications of the fresh gel. If you melt 1½ ounces (42g) cocoa butter with 4 ounces (115g) soybean oil and add 1 ounce (28g) aloe gel and mix all together you will have an ointment which can be used not only for eczema but for any skin which is dry and irritable. The addition of a small quantity of water in which comfrey root has been boiled up will make the ointment even better.

When smeared over the skin the gel will act as a suntan lotion. If you have been unwise enough to allow your skin to burn, apply the gel.

There are now many commercial preparations for the nourishment of both skin and hair made from aloe gel.

ANGELICA—Holy Ghost, Lungwort, Garden Angelica

Botanical name: *Angelica archangelica*
Family: *Umbelliferae*
Parts used: Root, seeds and herb

Angelica is a common garden plant in temperate areas and grows wild in other

Verbena (perennial)
Yarrow (perennial)

HERBS THAT MAKE ATTRACTIVE HOUSE PLANTS

Balm (perennial)
Basil (annual)
Borage (annual)
Burnet (perennial)
Chervil (biennial)
Lavender (perennial)
Marjoram (perennial)
Rosemary (perennial)
Sage (perennial)
Tarragon (perennial)
Verbena (perennial)

These are not showy plants but can look very pleasant when used in a massed arrangement with more strongly colored pot plants.

SWEET-SCENTED HERBS

Angelica (perennial)
Balm (perennial)
Basil (annual)
Bergamot (perennial)
Burnet (perennial)
Chamomile (perennial)
Dill (perennial)
Fennel (perennial)

parts of the world.

The garden plant is a tall biennial with glossy green leaves and umbels of sweet-scented yellowish-white flowers followed by seed-heads like those of the sunflower. It makes a good back-of-the-border plant and will happily self-seed provided there is some shade.

CULINARY USE

The aromatic seeds are used to flavor liqueurs such as Benedictine and Chartreuse. The dried leafstalks preserved with sugar can be bought as a cake decoration.

HOME-CANDIED ANGELICA

Eating this candy could cause a dislike for intoxicating liquor; the information can be treated as either advice or warning.

Boil short lengths of 2-year-old stems until tender. Strip off outer skin then boil the insides carefully until they become green but not soggy. Drain. Weigh. Cover with sugar equal to the weight of the stems and leave overnight. Boil until syrup becomes clear, drain stems, dust with fine sugar and dry on very low heat in oven. Store upright in glass jar and seal tight.

Finely chopped young angelica leaves add flavor to cottage and cream cheese and cheesecake. Make an herb punch by pouring a quart (liter) of boiling water over 1 ounce (30g) chopped angelica root, add brandy or rum to taste and serve with lemon slices.

Do not waste angelica stems, they can be made into a fine liqueur.

ANGELICA LIQUEUR

Weigh up one pound (450g) angelica stalks and cut them into short lengths. Put them into a jar containing about 2½ cups (600mL) brandy and add some mixed spice, leave for 3–4 weeks in a warm, sunny place. Add ½ pound (225g) granulated sugar dissolved in just enough water to make a clear solution. Strain through muslin cloth at least twice, then bottle. Leave for at least a week before using as a liqueur or flavoring for fresh fruit salads or stewed fruit.

MEDICINAL USE: Stimulant, carminative, diuretic, tonic.

An infusion of the leaves makes a tonic tea for colds and rheumatic chills and will bring on perspiration. Use ⅔ ounce (20g) chopped root or ½ ounce (15g) seeds to 4 cups (1L) boiling water. The sweet-scented stalk can be chewed to relieve stomachic wind. The dried root made into a tea is good for the appetite, will aid digestion and assist the anemic.

ANISE — Aniseed

Botanical name: *Pimpinella anisum*
Family: *Umbelliferae*
Parts used: Seeds and leaves

Given gentle warmth, shelter, lime in the soil and a hot sun when seeds are ripening, this native of the Middle East and the Mediterranean area will flourish quite happily. It is a low-growing dainty annual with feathery leaves and yellowish-white flowers that grow in umbels; the seeds are ribbed and hairy. Propagation is from seed but the seedlings do not readily transplant.

CULINARY USE

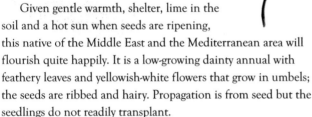

Try the chopped leaves, sparingly, in salads. Fish soup, applesauce, bread and confectionary can all be made more flavorsome by a judicious addition of the dried seeds.

MEDICINAL USE: Carminative and pectoral.

The dried seeds are so full of protein that regular intake will increase the breast milk of nursing mothers and avoid the depletion of their energy. Also good in cases of low blood pressure.

To cleanse the palate and ease digestion chew some dried seeds after a meal or make a drink by steeping a dessertspoonful of crushed seeds in 2½ cups (600mL) boiling water for 10 minutes.

Commercial cough medicines, lozenges, toothpastes, ointments, soaps and insect repellents all make use of anise.

COSMETIC USE

Girls desperate to remove freckles should try bathing them away with an infusion made from the feathery, delicate leaves.

Lavender (perennial)
Lovage (perennial)
Marjoram (perennial)
Sage (perennial)
Tansy (perennial)
Thyme (perennial)
Yarrow (perennial)

HERBS THAT ATTRACT BEES

Balm (perennial)
Basil (annual)
Bergamot (perennial)
Borage (annual)
Catmint (perennial)
Fennel (perennial)
Lavender (perennial)
Rosemary (perennial)
Sage (perennial)
Thyme (perennial)

Color is always important in a garden and while herbs do not have particularly large flowers they can, when massed, be used to great effect.

HERBS WITH BLUE FLOWERS

Aconite	Hyssop
Borage	Lavender
Chicory	Sage
Fennel	

ANISE — STAR

Botanical name: *Illicium verum*
Family: *Magnoliaceae*

This is a completely different plant—a small evergreen with pale bark and tiny many-petalled yellow flowers which are followed by star-shaped fruits. Grown only in China, the attractive fruits (which have a clean anise taste) can be bought dried for use in cooking, etc.

ARNICA — Leopard's Bane

Botanical name: *Arnica montana*
Family: *Compositae*
Parts used: Root and flowers
Poisonous herb

This northern hemisphere perennial plant has yellow, daisy-like flower which rise on slender 10-12 inches (25-30cm) stalks from a rosette of ground-hugging leaves; the root is a rhizome, the seeds and seed capsules are hairy. The plant is poisonous.

MEDICINAL USE: Stimulant, wound healer.

The flowers and root are widely used in tincture as a local application for the relief of bruises, swellings and sprains. Internal dosage is efficacious but should only be taken under medical supervision. However, homoeopathic preparations made from the plant can be taken quite safely.

ARROWROOT

Botanical name: *Maranta arudinaceae*
Family: *Marantaceae*
Part used: Root

This tall perennial native of South America has creamy flowers and pretty leaves but is most valuable for its root. It is useless to attempt to grow the plant in anything but a tropical climate.

CULINARY USE

The starchy powder obtained from the dried root has long been used as both invalid and baby food which will thicken warm milk and provide an easily digestible calcium-rich drink. It is preferable to flour as a thickener for puddings an sauces because it is more economical in use and cooks very quickly.

MEDICINAL USE: Demulcent.

The natives of South America used to pound up the fleshly root and apply it to wounds caused by poisoned arrows. A warm poultice applied to insect bites or simple but painful wounds will give quick relief.

When other foods are too difficult to digest, a warm milky arrowroot drink or pudding will be accepted by the system and act as a soother in cases of urinary or bowel inflammation.

HERBS WITH RED FLOWERS

Bergamot

HERBS WITH ORANGE FLOWERS

Calendula
Nasturtium
Tansy

HERBS WITH YELLOW FLOWERS

Arnica
Chamomile
Nasturtium

Many people think that all herbs must have sun to grow well but quite a number will tolerate a reasonably shady spot.

HERBS THAT CAN TAKE SHADE

Aconite
Angelica
Balm
Chervil
Comfrey
Mint
Parsley
Tarragon

All herbs need a well-

BALM—Sweet Balm, Lemon Balm, Honey Plant, Bee Herb

Botanical name: *Melissa offincinalis*
Family: *Labiatae*
Part used: Leaves

This easy-to-grow perennial garden herb is hardy, spreading and untidy. The crushed green, nettle-shaped leaves give off a pleasant lemon-mint fragrance; the flowers are small and pale. The plant will tolerate poor, light soil and will rampage in a rich moist one in both shady and sunny spots. Propagation is from seed, root division or cuttings.

CULINARY USE

The leaves can be used fresh or dried for flavoring salads, vinegars, stuffings, soups, puddings, wine cups and fruit drinks.

MEDICINAL USE: Carminative, febrifuge, sedative.

Tea made from the leaves gives a clean-tasting drink comforting to sufferers from colds, fevers or headaches. It brings on gentle perspiration.

An infusion of ⅔ ounce (20g) leaves in 4 cups (1L) boiling water allowed to stand for 10-15 minutes is useful in cupful doses for the relief of menstrual cramps and troubled digestion, and is also good for low blood pressure.

The bruised fresh leaves applied to a wound as an emergency measure will prevent infection.

IN THE HOME

The leaves hold their perfume will and help a potpourri to remain fragrant.

IN THE GARDEN

Bees are so attracted to this plant that beekeepers have been known to rub hives with the leaves in order to increase the size of the colony.

BASIL — Sweet Basil

Botanical name: *Ocimum basilicum*
Family: *Labiatae*
Part used: Leaves

In hot climates basil can be grown as a perennial, in cooler ones it is better treated as an annual.

The plant grows to about 20 inches (50cm) high with spikes of purplish-white flowers and leaves, which can be differently colored and differently flavored; all flavors are spicy and pleasant. Sow outdoors in the heat, in more temperate climates sow the seeds indoors or certainly under shelter, and transplant the seedlings when the weather has settled. Pinch out the growing tips to promote bushy growth and when picking for drying take the top portion of the stem and leave the lower to grow on and make a later crop.

CULINARY USE

The leaves, fresh or dried, can be used to flavor almost any savory dish but basil has a particular affinity with the tomato. Sprinkle the finely chopped leaves on thinly sliced tomato and add French dressing.

Finely chop basil sprigs, parsley leaves and stalks, and garlic; add olive oil and store the mixture in a covered pot in the refrigerator to be used in savory dishes. But best of all, make some Pesto sauce!

drained soil and only a few are really happy if the soil is continually moist.

HERBS THAT CAN TAKE A MOIST SOIL

Angelica
Bergamot
Lady's Mantle
Lovage
Mint
Parsley
Pennyroyal

HERBS THAT CAN TAKE A DRY SOIL

Agrimony
Arnica
Borage
Burnet
Chamomile
Chicory
Chives
Fennel
Lavender
Rosemary
Sage
Santolina
Thyme
Yarrow

The number of herbs that can be used in the treatment of

PESTO SAUCE

This traditional sauce is stirred into pasta or a vegetable soup just before serving.
Ingredients

2½ ounces (75g) chopped basil leaves

2 or 3 garlic cloves

2½ ounces (75g) grated Parmesan cheese

About one-third teacup olive oil

Some pine-nuts or walnuts (these grated nuts are optional so make 2 batches, one with and one without, to determine your preference)

Method

Using a mortar and pestle, pound together the basil leaves, nuts and garlic with salt to taste. Stir in the grated cheese then add the oil very, very gradually and stir the mixture well with a wooden spoon. Use immediately or store in the refrigerator.

MEDICINAL USE

The vehemence with which the ancients disagreed with each other about the use of basil is comical. Experience has shown that sniffing it is unlikely to cause scorpions to breed in the brain, and whether or not it is an aphrodisiac is still open to question, but what is certain is that a snuff made from powdered basil will clear the sinuses of catarrh sufferers and a tea made from the leaves and flowering tips will "settle" an agitated nervous system. Five grams of leaves to 32 ounces (100g) boiling water taken after meals is the recommended dosage.

HOUSEHOLD USE

A pot of basil on the windowsill will deter flies.

IN THE GARDEN

Bees love basil. Aphids, white fly and the fruit fly hate it. A border of basil near growing tomatoes will help the fruit to resist disease and give it added flavor.

BAY — Laurel, Sweet Bay

Botanical name: *Laurus nobilis*
Family: *Lauraceae*
Parts used: Leaves and berries

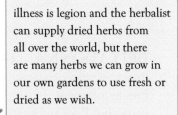

This handsome shrub will grow
to 30 feet (9m) high in the warmer
parts of the world and the yellowish, green-white flowers
growing in the stem axils are followed by small purplish-black
berries. Although the plant will grow well in cooler parts, it is
unlikely to bloom. This will not matter as the shiny, evergreen
leaves are the most important part.

Propagation is from cuttings. Given a light but well-
composted soil, a sheltered sunny position and protection
from frost, the shrub will grow slowly but strongly in the open
garden or in a tub as a specimen plant.

CULINARY USE

The leaves, fresh or dried, are used to give flavor to meat,
fish and vegetable dishes as well as to sweet puddings.

MEDICINAL USE: Diuretic.

The pulped berries produce an oil that makes a liniment
for bruises and sprains. This oil is only safe for external
application. A tea made from the leaves will ease the misery of
an over-indulgence in alcohol and rid the body of excess water.

HOUSEHOLD USE

A bay leaf or two kept in containers of flour and other
farinaceous food will keep weevils away.

illness is legion and the herbalist
can supply dried herbs from
all over the world, but there
are many herbs we can grow in
our own gardens to use fresh or
dried as we wish.

GARDEN HERBS WITH MEDICINAL USE

Agrimony
Angelica
Anise
Arnica
Balm
Bay
Blessed Thistle
Burdock
Calendula
Caraway
Centaury
Chamomile
Chicory
Comfrey
Dandelion
Dill
Fennel
Garlic
Horehound
Lovage
Marjoram
Nettle
Parsley
Rosemary

BELLADONNA — Deadly Nightshade

Botanical name: *Atropa belladonna*
Family: *Solanaceae*
Parts used: Root and leaves
Poisonous herb

This plant is of medium height with dark green oval leaves
and purple bell-shaped flowers, which are succeeded by shiny
black berries. A wild plant native to central and southern
Europe, it is cultivated for medicinal use. All parts of the plant are poisonous and if ever there
was a plant to leave alone as far as home use goes, this is it!

MEDICINAL USE: Diuretic, sedative.

The drug atropine is extracted from the juice of the root and leaves and is useful, under
medical supervision, as a diuretic or sedative. One of the alkaloids extracted from the
root is used to dilate the pupils of the eye so that optometrists and doctors can make an
examination. Nowadays it is used responsibly, but in the Middle Ages ladies used the extract
of the herb to enlarge their pupils in the odd belief that such enlargement would make their
eyes look more beautiful.

BERGAMOT (RED) — Bee Balm,
Indian Plume, Oswego Tea

Botanical name: *Monarda didyma*
Family: *Labiatae*
Part used: Leaves

A handsome plant with fragrant leaves and whorls of scented red
flowers rather like those of the honeysuckle. It is a splendid garden plant
that will grow to over 3 feet (1m) in height given plenty of water.

Rue
Tansy
Thyme
Yarrow

To keep the plant at its best it should be dug up every now and then, the old roots pulled out and discarded and the younger roots replanted. Since it throws out runners, it can spread quickly if it likes the conditions.

CULINARY USE

The leaves give an added flavor to wine cups or tea made from other blander-tasting herbs.

The young leaves and scarlet flowers make a delicious and attractive addition to salads and fruit drinks; pork dishes taste better if a leaf or so of bergamot is included, and scalding milk poured over a dessertspoonful of dried leaves makes a very pleasant nightcap.

MEDICINAL USE

The leaves, which contain thymol, a powerful antiseptic oil, can be used in infusion as a gargle for a sore, inflamed throat.

COSMETIC USE

Bergamot oil forms the basis of some commercial suntan lotions.

HOUSEHOLD USE

The dried flowers and leaves hold their fragrance so well that no potpourri is complete without them.

BORAGE — Bee Bread

Botanical name: *Borago officinalis*
Family: *Boraginaceae*
Parts used: Flowers, stems and leaves

Borage is an attractive annual plant with hairy stems and hairy, wrinkled leaves with star-shaped blue flowers in clusters. It will self-sow even in poor ground, enjoys sun, will tolerate some cold but does not transplant well. Bees love it.

CULINARY USE

The young raw leaves are good in salads or added to fruit drinks. Their flavor is fresh and cucumber-like. The flowers can be candied and used as cake decorations or eaten raw.

CANDIED BORAGE FLOWERS

Brush the freshly opened flowers with the white of an egg then dust with caster sugar. Some people leave the flowers to dry naturally on waxed paper, others use low heat in a conventional oven for a long time or low heat in a microwave oven for considerably less time. In any case, be certain the flowers are quite dry and crisp before you store them in a closed glass container.

MEDICINAL USE: Demulcent, diuretic, stimulant.

Since it has been established how rich the plant is in mineral salts, potassium and calcium, the ancients were clearly not just being fanciful when they claimed that borage "maketh the mind glad and driveth away all sadness." The modern explanation is that it increases the body's adrenalin output.

An infusion made from the leaves and flowers will act as a blood cleanser, tonic, laxative and a cough soother. Use 1 ounce (30g) herb to 22 cups (600mL) boiling water and take in wineglass doses 3 times a day.

HOUSEHOLD USE

The flowers look so pretty when dried; they are often found in flower pictures made by using dried stems, leaves, flower heads, etc.

IN THE GARDEN

It will attract bees—always a bonus. It may not be the most decorative plant in the world because it always seems to flop, but the intense blue of the pretty flowers, a color too seldom found in the garden, makes it welcome.

BURDOCK—Beggars' Buttons

Botanical name: *Arctium lappa*
Family: *Compositae*
Parts used: Root and leaves

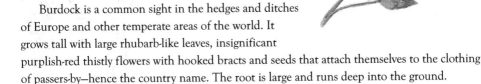

Burdock is a common sight in the hedges and ditches of Europe and other temperate areas of the world. It grows tall with large rhubarb-like leaves, insignificant purplish-red thistly flowers with hooked bracts and seeds that attach themselves to the clothing of passers-by—hence the country name. The root is large and runs deep into the ground.

CULINARY USE

The young leaves can be added to salads and the young root eaten boiled and buttered. The leaves are slightly bitter, the root slightly sweet. Used with dandelion, it was a favorite spring tonic. Many people will remember the tangy taste of "Dandelion and Burdock."

MEDICINAL USE: Alterative, diuretic.

A decoction made from the roots and seeds provides one of the best blood cleansers in the herbal kingdom.

Burdock is a "skin herb" par excellence. A decoction of a handful of chopped leaves to 22 cups (600mL) water, boiled for 10 minutes, can be used when cool as a face wash in cases of acne, impetigo, psoriasis or, when warm, on boils and carbuncles. One ounce (28g) root boiled in 32 cups (850mL) water until liquid is reduced by almost a third, can be taken in cup-sized doses for the same complaints. A poultice made with the pulped leaves will alleviate the pain of arthritic joints, sprains and bruises. Burdock root contains insulin and can therefore reduce the blood sugar of the diabetic. A decoction made by boiling 2 ounces (60g) fresh root in 22 cups (600mL) water and taken in cupful doses 3 times a day is recommended.

COSMETIC USE

A steam bath made with burdock leaves is good for any skin, particularly for "problem" ones.

CAPSICUM — Pepper, Chili Pepper

Botanical name: *Capsicum annuum*
Family: *Solanaceae*
Part used: Fruit

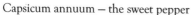

There are many different varieties of the Capsicum family: from large, sweet-tasting peppers to the small, fiery-tasting ones. All belong to the potato family, which includes Belladonna (poisonous) and the tomato. Originally natives of Central America, capsicum can now be found growing in both very warm and temperate parts of the world.

Capsicum annuum — the sweet pepper

This plant is an annual with a bushy habit, thick stems, shiny, slightly-toothed leaves, small white flowers (very like those of the potato), followed by large fruits which turn red as they ripen.

Capsicum frutescens—chili pepper, cayenne

This plant is a perennial similar to the sweet pepper but with small leaves and much small fruits, very fiery to the taste. The seeds of both varieties are acrid and should be carefully removed before the fruit is used.

Both varieties can be grown from seed and need a warm, well-drained sandy soil and sun while the fruit is ripening.

CULINARY USE

The flesh of the sweet pepper is eaten either raw or cooked and is a valuable source of Vitamin C. It is also dried and ground to make Paprika pepper and used very widely in Hungarian cookery.

The flesh of the chili pepper is used fresh or dry in the typically hot dishes from Mexico and India. The dried fruits are used for pickling or to give flavor to chutneys, etc. and are the main ingredient in the popular Tabasco sauce.

MEDICINAL USE

The raw flesh of the sweet pepper will stop a wound from bleeding and, made into a poultice, will reduce inflammation and ease the pain of rheumatism, arthritis and pleurisy.

The ground dried fruits of the chili pepper are stimulant, tonic and disinfectant. A light infusion will aid circulation and give the body warmth and act as a gargle—try a little Tabasco sauce dissolved in warm water. Since the alkaloid contained in the fruit is an irritant, over-enthusiastic use is not recommended, but used sensibly it will aid the treatment of all conditions where reduction of inflammation and purification of the blood are prerequisites. Sprinkled over a slow-burning fire, the pepper will fumigate a sickroom.

CARAWAY

Botanical name: *Carum carvi*
Family: *Umbelliferae*
Parts used: Root, leaves and seed

Feathery leaves and umbels of creamy-white flowers on long stalks make this biennial a delightful garden plant for all temperate areas. It is undemanding as to soil, will readily self-seed, but does not transplant well. It likes full sun.

CULINARY USE

Travelers to Europe, particularly Germany and Austria, will have recognized the distinctive flavor in Kummel, rye bread and sauerkraut. The strange spicy taste has been popular with man ever since the Stone Age.

The roots can be boiled and eaten, the young leaves used raw in salads, but the dried seed is the most used part of the plant. Try a pinch or two in soups, vegetables, savory dishes and with the greasier meats and poultry. "Seed Cake" has been a favorite since Victorian times despite the cries of: "They get under my plate!"

SEED CAKE

Ingredients
6½ ounces (185g) butter or margarine
½ cup sugar
3 eggs

2 teaspoons caraway seeds
1½ cups self-raising flour
¼ cup milk

Method

Cream butter and sugar. Separate eggs and beat whites until firm. Lightly beat yolks and add carefully to whites and creamed mixture. Gradually add flour, caraway seeds and milk and stir well.

Place mixture in cake tin, sprinkle with more seeds and bake in moderate heat for about 55 minutes or until cake is golden and firm to the touch.

MEDICINAL USE: Carminative, stimulant.

A tea made from the leaves will settle an upset stomach; try small doses on fretful, colicky babies. It also acts as a general tonic.

The seeds, when chewed after a meal, will sweeten the breath and aid digestion.

CARDAMOM

Botanical name: *Elettaria cardamomum*
Family: *Zingiberaceae*
Part used: Seed

The whole plant has the look of the ginger family to which it belongs. The stems are tall with large leaves and shorter flowering stem. The yellow and blue flowers are followed by capsules containing small round seeds, which are picked before they are ripe and dried slowly to retain their valuable properties. Cardamom, which will only grow in hot climates, is best propagated by root division although it does reasonably well from seed if time is no object.

CULINARY USE

The highly flavored spice made from the ground seed has been used in its native India since long before the Christian era. Today, a typical Indian dish is almost certain to taste of it.

The seeds are used whole in fruit drinks and pickles, and ground as flavoring for bread, cakes, puddings, pancakes, stewed fruits, fresh fruit salad, hamburgers, roast meats, sausages and curries. They are often bought in the pod.

CARDAMOM CARROTS

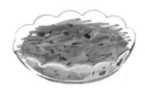

Ingredients

1¾ ounces (50g) carrots cut into small thin strips

1½ ounces (40g) brown sugar

1½ ounces (40g) margarine or butter

9 cardamom seeds (whole)

grated rinds 1 orange

Method

Cook the carrot strips with a little salt until tender, either on top of the stove or in a microwave oven. Drain.

Melt butter and sugar together, stir well, add grated orange rind and the crushed cardamoms, heat carefully until sugar has dissolved. Pour over carrots and stir well. Freshly ground black pepper can be added.

MEDICINAL USE: Carminative, stomachic.

A tea made from the seed will stimulate appetite, aid digestion and eliminate wind.

CASCARA SAGRADA—Sacred Bark, Bearberry, Californian Buckthorn

Botanical name: *Thamnus purshiana*
Family: *Simarubaceae*
Part used: Bark

This tall shrub is native to California and British Columbia and its value lies in its dried, furrowed, leather-smelling bark.

MEDICINAL USE

Fluid extracts of the bark are sold as purgatives and intestinal tonics. Bark bought from an herbalist for home use should be dark brown; the lighter-colored younger bark can cause griping.

A tea made by pouring boiling water over a small quantity of bark should be left to stand until cool; a small cupful drunk at bedtime will relieve constipation and is not habit-forming. The tea will also help the action of the liver and ease the inflammation and irritation of piles.

CATMINT—Catnip

Botanical name: *Nepeta cataria*
Family: *Labiatae*
Parts used: Leaves and flowers

Catmint, with its velvety, heart-shaped gray-green leaves and pale lavender-colored flowers, is a perennial plnat which has been a long-time favorite in the flower borders of gardens of warm to temperate climates. It grows to about 3 feet (1m) in height and will straggle unless controlled. It tolerates both sun and shade. Its main attraction is that, apart from looking pretty, the bruised leaves and flowers give off a delicate fragrance.

Cats love it. Our own cat rolls in it at every available opportunity undeterred by our shouts of rage at the sight of the flattened plants. Cut it back hard after flowering and it will flower again. Propagation by layering or root division is easy; growing from seed is a lengthier process but not difficult.

MEDICINAL USE: Carminative, tonic, diaphoretic

The bruised fresh leaves applied locally will reduce the inflammation of piles. A tea made from the leaves and flowers will not only ease colds and chills by inducing perspiration but will also relieve stomach cramp, hiccups and flatulence and help to bring on delayed menstruation.

It is also said to be good for neuralgia.

An enema made from catmint tea is reputed to have the ability to cope with difficult or suppressed urination even when all else has failed.

COSMETIC USE

The leaves and flowers simmered in vinegar will darken mousy hair and promote its growth.

HOUSEHOLD USE

Rats hate it.

IN THE GARDEN

Bees love it. A tea made from the leaves and flowers when cooled is good for watering plants and will give them protection against insect attack.

CELANDINE

There are two celandines and it is important to distinguish one from the other. They look superficially alike but belong to different families and have different properties.

GREATER CELANDINE—Celandine Poppy, Felonwort, Tetterwort

Botanical name: *Cheliodonium majus*
Family: *Papaveraceae*

In its native state the Greater Celandine grows in Europe, North Africa and parts of Asia, in shady, stony places against walls or on wasteland. It was introduced by colonists to other parts of the world.

The plant has downy, heavily divided leaves on downy stems and the four-petalled yellow flowers, which grow in clusters at the end of a long stem, are followed by 2-inch (5cm) long pods that contain small black seeds. The thick underground part of the stems and the tall stems above ground will produce a milky, poisonous juice when cut.

This juice can be used to remove warts and corns but that is as far as home use of the plant should go. Homoeopathic practitioners will prescribe safe doses for congestion of the liver, dropsy and "stones."

LESSER CELANDINE—Pilewort, Figwort

Botanical name: *Ranunculus ficaria*
Family: *Ranunculaceae*

This plant has thick, glossy, toothed, ivy or heart-shaped leaves, golden star-shaped flowers on short stems and it prefers marshy land. The low-growing leaves can carpet an area very quickly. If you pull up the roots you will find small whitish bulbs, which make it obvious why the plant earned the name "pilewort."

As a remedy for piles the roots can be crushed, mixed with lanoline (or even butter or margarine), heated gently, stirred well and then strained and the subsequent ointment stored in a covered pot for use when piles are painful.

Alternately, q ounce (20g) roots boiled in 22 cups (600mL) water make a decoction that can be used warm as an external application for piles, or drunk cooled in cupful doses no more than twice a day.

CENTAURY — Common Centaury, Feverwort

Botanical name: *Erytbraeae centaurium*
Family: *Gentianaceae*
Part used: All the plant above ground

This wild herb grows in the woods and fields of Europe and Britain and other temperate and sub-tropical climates. It can be either annual or biennial, depending on the heat needed to produce flowers and seeds. The oval leaves grow close to the ground in a rosette form, above which lift pretty pink flowers.

MEDICINAL USE: Tonic, stomachic.

Centaury makes a "bitters" drink which aids digestion. An infusion of 1 ounce (30g) leaves to 22 cups (600mL) boiling water taken in wineglassful doses will relieve the pain and wind suffered after a heavy meal. A weak infusion makes a good eye bath for conjunctivitis.

CHAMOMILE

Botanical name: Matricaria chamomilla, Anthemis nobilis
Family: Compositae
Parts used: Flowers and herb

The best known of the species of chamomile are the German (matricaria chamomilla) and the Roman (anthemis nobilis). They both have feathery divided leaves, small, white daisy-like flowers with a yellow center and a pungent scent.

The German, the true or wild chamomile, is a tall annual that grows by the wayside and self-seeds freely. The Roman is a low-growing perennial with strong runners, which form a mat. It can be distinguished by examination of the yellow center of the flower; it is hollow. If you choose to grow the German chamomile in the garden, be prepared to find it everywhere; gathering most of the flowers before they go to seed will help to keep it under control. The Roman chamomile can be grown to make a thick scented lawn, which can be mown and rolled like a grass lawn. All the flower heads should be snipped off before they can make any height. Look out for the non-flowering variety Chamomilla nobile which will make an excellent lawn once the tedious planting-out of seedlings and the weeding, necessary in the early stages, have been overcome.

MEDICINAL USE

A tea made from the dried flowers is a good sedative and useful for feverish colds. An infusion of 1¾ ounce (50g) dried flowers to 2½ cups (600mL) boiling water can be used as an antiseptic, inhalant or gargle. The flowers when soaked in hot water make a good poultice for boils and abscesses, slow-healing wounds, and rheumaticky joints.

COSMETIC USE

A rinse for blonde hair can be made from a strong infusion of dried or fresh flowers, and a bath oil by steeping the crushed flowers in baby oil for 3 weeks in a warm place.

USE IN THE GARDEN

The chamomiles give strength to nearby plants and keep many flying insects at bay.

CHERVIL — Poor Man's Tarragon

Botanical name: *Anthriscus cerifolium*
Family: *Umbelliferae*
Part used: Leaves

Chervil has pale green, lacy, sweet-scented leaves and small white flowers. This annual plant can be difficult to grow as it dislikes heat, will not tolerate frost, does not easily transplant and is so delicate it must be handled with care at all times—it does not even dry particularly well. However, used fresh, it makes a delightful culinary herb which enhances the flavor of a dish without imposing too much of its own. It also has good medicinal qualities.

CULINARY USE

The light aniseed-like flavor of the leaves is very pleasant in a salad and as an additive to meat and fish dishes. Chopped hard-boiled eggs are livened by a sprinkling of chopped chervil.

A clean-tasting soup that is good either hot or cold can be made using chervil.

SOUP

Ingredients
1 heaping dessertspoon chopped leaves
3 tablespoons butter or margarine
1 large potato
2½ cups (625mL) hot chicken stock
cream
salt and ground black pepper

Method

Sauté the chervil in the hot butter or margarine, fry potato until soft, add stock and seasoning, stir well, cook gently for 20 minutes not allowing the mixture to come to the boil. Stir in cream just before serving. Some people like to add a sprinkling of freshly grated nutmeg at the last minute.

A simple chervil sauce can be made by mixing fresh, finely chopped leaves into thickened cream well seasoned with black pepper and a little salt. Good for chicken dishes.

MEDICINAL USE

Chervil tea is a wonderful tonic for both nerves and brain and doesn't taste bad either. If you think your memory is failing, try it! It is also good for lowering high blood pressure. **Note:** When buying a chervil plant ask for it by its botanical name to avoid confusion with other chervils.

CHICKWEED

Botanical name: *Stellaria media*
Family: *Caryophyllaceae*
Part used: Herb

An annual weed with smooth succulent stems and small, white, star-like flowers, the chickweed is surely known to every gardener. It is an easy weed to eradicate but can be put to good use.

MEDICINAL USE: Tonic, demulcent.

An infusion of the leaves and stems makes a good, slightly salty-tasting tonic drink, for the plant is rich in iron and copper. This is why fresh chickweed is so good for caged birds. The infusion also makes a good bath for sore eyes. Strain well before use. The same infusion with the addition of a little lemon juice and honey will relieve congested bowels.

The fresh leaves make a good poultice for ulcers that take too long to heal, eczema, etc.

CHICORY

Botanical name: *Chicorium intybus*
Family: *Compositae*
Part used: Root

Chicory, a wild plant in Europe and Asia, has long been naturalized in other parts of the world.

It is a medium-sized perennial with pointed, toothed leaves and blue flowers, rather like those of the dandelion, which grow in the axils of the leaves at the top of the stems.

The leaves taste bitter and to make them acceptable as a vegetable or salad herb they are blanched by covering the plant with a layer of sand. The root, which can grow quite large, is used dried, roasted and ground as an additive to coffee or to provide an infusion that will stimulate the production of bile and ease digestive upsets.

CULINARY USE

Do not soak the root in water or it will become bitter. Do not boil, just braise with butter and lemon juice and serve with white sauce or a mild cheese sauce.

CHIVES

Botanical name: *Allium shoenoprasum*
Family: *Liliaceae*
Part used: Leaves

Chives are the "babies" of the onion family but, unlike
the onion, they are grown more for their leaves than their
bulbs. The perennial plants grow in clusters and their fine
upright leaves and delicate pompon flowers which can range
from mauve to pink make them an attractive border-edging
plant even if no use is felt for their excellent culinary and
medicinal properties.

They enjoy a rich, moist soil and warmth but are likely to
die back and not reappear until spring if the winter weather
is too cold; they will also "yellow" if the soil does not contain

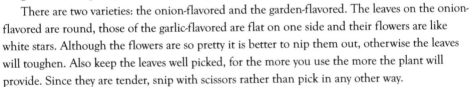

sufficient nutrients. They can be grown from seed but since the bulbs increase in number with
the growth of the plant, division is much quicker and simpler.

There are two varieties: the onion-flavored and the garden-flavored. The leaves on the onion-
flavored are round, those of the garlic-flavored are flat on one side and their flowers are like
white stars. Although the flowers are so pretty it is better to nip them out, otherwise the leaves
will toughen. Also keep the leaves well picked, for the more you use the more the plant will
provide. Since they are tender, snip with scissors rather than pick in any other way.

CULINARY USE

Chives do not dry very successfully but quick-freeze very well. Small quantities wrapped in foil
and kept in a plastic box in the freezer will see you through winter in case your plants die down.

As far as fresh chives go, if you like onion or garlic flavor it can be a case of chopped chives
with everything savory—from cream cheese, vegetables, soups, omelets, scrambled eggs, and
salads; used as garnish they are more likely to be eaten than the mandatory parsley sprig and,
since they contain iron and sulfur, add to the value of the food.

Left-over potatoes, mashed, well-seasoned, with the addition of chopped chives can, with a little butter added if needed, be shaped into cakes, lightly floured and then fried to make a savory and nourishing extra to an unexciting meal. Always cut up chives with scissors as a knife will bruise them.

MEDICINAL USE

While chives, per se, are not used as a medicine, the sulfur they contain (while less than that of the onion) is valuable, and garlic chives in particular give protection against contagious diseases.

IN THE GARDEN

A border of chives, again particularly the garlic-flavored ones, will give rosebushes protection against aphids and a chives "tea" made by pouring boiling water over a handful of chopped leaves can be used, when cooled, for feeding gooseberry bushes and cucumber plants which are showing signs of mildew.

Apples are said to be less liable to scab if chives are growing nearby.

CINNAMON

Botanical name: *Cinnamomium zeylanicum*
Family: *Lauraceae*
Part used: Bark

Cinnamon is a tall, thick, evergreen tree native to Sri Lanka. It will grow in other tropical climates. The bark is the most important part of the tree for, when ground, it provides a sweet spice valued for both culinary and medicinal usage. It was one of the spices carried by the caravans of the merchants in the ancient days when monopoly of the spice trade dictated the rise and fall of empires.

The leaves are pointed, smooth and tough and the small, creamy-white flowers are followed by dark blue berries. The bark peels off in thin curling quills and the best spice is obtained from the young shoots.

CULINARY USE

The powdered bark is used as a flavoring for cakes and desserts as well as for chicken and pork dishes. The "sticks" can be added to the pickling vinegar along with other spices. Fruit punches and mulled wine are improved by the spicy but delicate flavor. The Dutch are particularly fond of cinnamon and use it mixed with sugar on cakes and biscuits.

CINNAMON TOAST

Mix ground cinnamon with sugar to taste, toast some thick slice of bread, butter will so that the toast is well soaked and spread the cinnamon and sugar over the top, pressing the mixture firmly into the bread.

QUICK SWEET

Ingredients

9 ounces (250g) cream cheese

2 tablespoons milk 3 tablespoons cream

Method

Mix cheese, milk and cream till smooth, add sugar and ground cinnamon to taste. Place in a dish or dishes and grate the chocolate on top. The sweet can either be served immediately or refrigerated until needed.

Try ground cinnamon sprinkled on tofu or lightly sprinkled over fresh fruit salad.

MEDICINAL USE: Stimulant, digestive, antiseptic.

A little cinnamon added to a cup of black tea will ease diarrhea.

Added to warm water a little ground cinnamon makes a good oral disinfectant and will sweeten the breath. It also provides a warming drink for a cold or a troubled digestion.

CLOVES

Botanical name: *Eugenia carophylla* **or** *aromatica*
Family: *Myrtaceae*
Part used: Flower buds

The evergreen clove tree is a native of the Molucca
Islands and will only grow in a hot country. Zanzibar is
now known as the "clove island" and the scent hangs
over the city much as the scent of the "maquis" hangs
over some Mediterranean islands.

The tree is tall and the flowers a clear red. They
are picked for drying while still in bud. If you nick the calyx of the flower with a fingernail
it exudes a pungent-smelling oil which the early alchemists were quick to realize makes an
excellent antiseptic.

The clove came to Europe in the early days of the "spice trade" but it had long been known
in China even then.

CULINARY USE

The cloves (the dried flower heads) are used to flavor stewed fruit—particularly apples or
pears—mulled wine, soups and meat dishes. An onion studded with cloves, added to a soup or
stew, should be removed before the dish is sent to the table.

Cloves are used for garnishing a ham for baking. The outside of the ham is deeply scored,
dried off with an application of flour rubbed well in, and the "diamond" or other pattern used
for scoring is then studded with cloves, glacé cherries and pieces of chopped canned pineapple.

Pickling vinegar is often spiced with cloves as with other spices. If the flavor is liked, bland
sauces can be enlivened with the addition of a few cloves.

MEDICINAL USE: Stimulant, carminative, antiseptic.

Oil of cloves applied to a hollow tooth will ease pain quite dramatically. Chewing a few
cloves will freshen the breath and ease nausea and persistent vomiting.

Clove tea made by pouring boiling water over no more than 3-4 cloves is also a useful carminative.

HOUSEHOLD USE

Insects do not like the clean strong smell of cloves. A pomander to hang in the wardrobe can be made by studding a ripe, thin-skinned orange with dried cloves, rolling it in a mixture of powdered orrisroot and powdered cinnamon and leaving it to dry for several weeks in a dark, dry place. Prettied up with a ribbon for hanging it not only gives off a good scent but also looks attractive.

COLTSFOOT—Coughwort, Horsehoof

Botanical name: *Tussilago farfara*
Family: *Compositae*
Parts used: Flowers and leaves

Coltsfoot is a weed. It grows in the poorest, heaviest soils quite happily in a temperate climate. The leaves are broad and hoof-shaped and very downy on the underside; the yellow daisy-like flowers turn into seeds that can be puffed away like dandelion "clocks." The perennial plant grows to only 14 inches (30cm) high and the curious thing about it is that the flowers bloom and die before the leaves appear. Coltsfoot has a long history of usefulness to mankind.

MEDICINAL USE: Dulmulcent, expectorant.

Tea made from the leaves should be strained to remove the downy hairs. This tea, 1 teaspoonful leaves to a cup of boiling water, is good for coughs and bronchitis and a raspy throat and can be used when cooled as a face-wash to minimize thread-veins.

Herbal tobaccos for asthmatics contain a significant amount of coltsfoot. If you would like to make your own herbal tobacco, try a mixture of dried thyme, rosemary, chamomile flowers, ground ivy, and wood betony with dried coltsfoot leaves in by far the heaviest proportion.

A primitive asthma remedy was to burn coltsfoot on a charcoal fire and to draw the smoke deep into the lungs.

COMFREY—Knitbone, Boneset, Blackwort
Botanic name: *Symphytum officinale*
Family: *Boraginaceae*
Parts used: Leaves and roots

Comfrey is a perennial plant native to Europe and the more temperate parts of Asia and will grow in any temperate area in any part of the world when given a moist and shady spot.

The hollow, hairy stems reach almost 3 feet (1m) in height and bear large, hairy, pointed leaves which decrease in size from the bottom of the stem upward. White flower spikes grow at the top of the stems and the large, wrinkled root is brownish-black.

Propagation from seed is a lengthy process and the more popular method is to cut off a section of root showing a "bud" and plant that. These root cuttings usually take easily and grow quickly and strongly.

CULINARY USE
The hairy leaves can be steamed and used as a vegetable although the taste is a little bitter for most palates. The chopped root can be added to chutney.

MEDICINAL USE: Demulcent, astringent, pectoral, vulnerary, styptic.

Comfrey's wonderful reputation rests largely on its ability to knit together broken bones and torn flesh. Nasty wounds, burns and scalds will heal without a scar if treated with a poultice made from the leaves, and the swellings of sprains and bruises will reduce. Oil the skin before applying the poultice to avoid irritation. Comfrey ointment, which can be bought very readily, is an excellent household first-aid for tired muscles, sore joints and the inflammation of rheumatism, etc.

The plant contains allantoin, which encourages the healthy granulation of tissue and can affect reparation both inside and outside the body. It was found that regular dosage of a large wineglassful of liquid, made by soaking 5 ounces (150g) chopped and well-bruised comfrey root in 4 cups (1L) of water for several hours, checked the erosion of stomach ulcers and encouraged new tissue to grow over the damages are. It is also good for colitis.

A decoction made by boiling 1 ounce (30g) chopped root in a liter of water for several minutes will, when taken in wineglassful does, help tonsillitis and pharyngitis—it can also be used as a gargle.

A tea brewed from the leaves and chopped roots not only makes a good cough mixture but will arrest internal bleeding of any sort. This tea should be taken fresh and not kept.

Comfrey is an herb which has been used and trusted for many, many years, so that when medical authorities lately prohibited the sale of comfrey made up into medicine for internal use, there was a great deal of amazement and resentment around. I understand—but please check this—that the decision that it was "unsafe" was based on the fact that rats being fed comfrey, as one-third of their diet, developed liver trouble. If they had been fed foxglove as one-third of their diet they would have been dead, but we have not heard that digitalis can no longer be taken for heart trouble!

The matter of taking comfrey as a medicine is something people must decide for themselves and is something worth looking into; it would be a pity if a valuable medicine were to be unobtainable in our generation, but fortunately the comfrey plant is easy to grow and there is still room for personal judgment and choice to be made.

CORIANDER

Botanical name: *Coriandrum sativum*
Family: *Umbelliferae*
Parts used: Leaves and seeds

This medium-sized annual with pretty green leaves and umbels of pinky-white flowers is a native of the warmer parts of Europe and southern Asia but will grow happily in any temperate part of the world provided it is given a light soil and plenty of sun.

When the seeds are unripe the whole plant has a rather unpleasant smell, but once the seeds ripen this changes to the scent that has made the dried seed a favorite spice. Propagation can be made from seed.

CULINARY USE

The seeds are used either whole or ground into a powder. If the flavor is liked, coriander can be added to cakes, stewed fruit, vegetables, and pork and ham dishes. The young leaves, used fresh, can be chopped and added to salads. If you make your own curry powder be sure to include coriander.

Coriander is used commercially as a flavoring for liqueurs and in perfume making.

COSTMARY – Alecost, Bible Leaf

Botanical name: *Chrysanthemum balsamita*
Family: *Compositae*
Part used: Leaves

Costmary is a perennial plant with long, narrow leaves and button-like yellow flowers, sometimes with tiny, white daisy-like petals. It has a minty, slightly bitter scent. It will grow in any temperate part of the world provided it has sun and can be propagated by division of the creeping roots. Since it spreads quickly the new plants should be given space.

CULINARY USE

The leaves were once widely used as a flavoring for home-brewed ale, today a very small amount of chopped leaf will be sufficient to enliven salads, stuffings and cooked vegetables.

MEDICINAL USE: Astringent, antiseptic.

An infusion made from the leaves will bring on menstruation and is said to make childbirth easier.

Crushed fresh leaves applied to insect stings will relieve the pain and tea made from the leaves makes a pleasant-tasting tonic drink.

COUCHGRASS — Twitch, Scutch, Dog's Grass

Botanical name: *Agropyron repens*
Family: *Graminaceae*
Part used: Root

This perennial is familiar to gardeners all over the temperate regions of the world as a bothersome weed which, once invading a lawn or garden, is difficult to eradicate. The root is a white, creeping rhizome which throws out stems that carry flat pointed leaves and sharp flower spikes. The smooth slender root has nodes about 12 inches (30cm) apart.

MEDICINAL USE: Diuretic and aperient.

The roots are rich in Vitamins A and B and minerals. Cut into short lengths, diced, and made into an infusion of 1 ounce (30g) root to 2½ cups (600mL) boiling water, wineglassful doses are prescribed in cases of feverishness, urinary and bladder complaints, renal colic and jaundice. The tea is also thought to be good for arteriosclerosis.

Cats and dogs show their good sense by eating this grass when they feel they should.

IN THE GARDEN

Since the root is so rich in food it should be chopped and added to the compost heap.

COWSLIP — Paigles, Our Lady's Keys

Botanical name: *Primula veris*
Family: *Primulaceae*
Parts used: Flowers and leaves

One of the best-loved of the English wild flowers, the cowslip grows in hedgerows and woods and is a herald of spring. The creamy-yellow flowers rise on slender stems from low-growing downy leaves. Introduced into the "wild" part of the garden, they are particularly lovely when growing with wild violets. The flower has a delicate fragrance.

CULINARY USE

The flowers, nipped from the stalk, make a salad garnish which can be eaten; the flavor is light and sweet. The dried flowers seem to lose some of their flavor.

Wine made from the flowers used to be one of the best-known and potent country drinks and, in spring, girls were eager to gather the flowers of the "paigle," for "distilled water from this herb of Venus taketh away spots and wrinkles and adds beauty exceedingly."

MEDICINAL USE

An infusion made from the flowers and leaves is laxative and diuretic but, possibly because of the tiny leaf hairs, can irritate the stomach, so should be used sparingly. It is also a gentle sedative with the ability to relieve cramp and giddiness.

COSMETIC USE

Strained cowslip tea is a good face-wash.

CUMIN

Botanical name: *Cuminium cyminum*
Family: *Umbelliferae*
Part used: Seeds

Cumin is an annual plant with feathery leaves, rather like those of the carrot, and umbels of pale flowers. A native of the Middle East, it will grow in other areas that are neither too warm nor too cold. Cumin is grown for its seed, which can be used alone as a food flavoring although it is best known as a component of curry powder.

CULINARY USE

Ground cumin makes a good seasoning for soups and stews—use in pinch-size additions to get the flavor right—and the crushed seed can be rubbed over beef or lamb before roasting. The whole seed can be added to the water in which vegetables are to be cooked. It is particularly good with cabbage or sprinkled over the top of cakes or cookies before cooking. The flavor has a clean sharpness and the scent of the seed is quite strong.

MEDICINAL USE

The crushed seeds can be added to any sort of poultice to aid local stimulation.

DANDELION

Botanical name: *Taraxacum officinalis*
Family: *Compositae*
Parts used: Leaves, roots, flowers and sap

There are few parts of the world where the dandelion is unknown. The golden-yellow tufted flowers and green-toothed leaves, the "puffball" seed-heads and the strong milky juice it produces make it impossible to ignore. Too often regarded as just a troublesome weed it is, in fact, one of the richest in the whole plant kingdom as it contains iron, copper, inulin, protein, fat, and a range of vitamins and mineral salts. Every home herb garden should contain a dandelion patch as the whole plant is medicinal as well as culinary.

CULINARY USE

The young leaves can be used in salads. If the taste is too bitter, blanch them. Boiled or steamed as a vegetable they make a healthy food but the taste may have to be acquired. Try a few chopped leaves in vegetable soups.

The flowers are used to make dandelion wine and the leaves, often used dried, in the making of herb beer, usually with burdock. The roots, roasted and ground, make a good coffee substitute for people who find coffee hard on the digestion and their ability to sleep.

An unusual decoration for salads can be made by freezing a single dandelion-head in each of the sections of an ice-cube tray. I only came across this once and though the cubes looked very handsome and made a good talking point, I remember that nobody knew what to do with the cubes, particularly when they started to melt! Use such cubes by all means but when the surprise and admiration begin to die, remove them at speed.

MEDICINAL USE: Diuretic, tonic, digestive.

And early spring dandelion "cure" which will rid the blood of impurities is made by boiling up 1 tablespoonful fresh, chopped root and leaves in half a cup of water and leaving it to cool. It should be made fresh, twice a day. It will stimulate the flow of urine, bile and gall and hence aid digestion and clear the skin, relieve constipation and help to remove the acids of rheumatism and gout, etc.

A decoction of the dried plant is also effective. Steep 1 ounce (30g) each of root and leaves in 4 cups (1L) water for 2 or 3 hours, bring the water just to the boil and then leave to cool. A cupful before meals 3 times a day is the recommended dosage.

Diabetics find dandelion tea a useful drink. The milky juice of the plant, applied regularly, is said to remove warts and corns.

COSMETIC USE

A good handful of young flowers, boiled up in 4 cups (1L) of water and then strained, can be used as a skin cleanser and is said to remove unwanted freckles.

DILL

Botanical name: *Anethum graveolens*
Family: *Umbelliferae*
Parts used: Leaves and seeds

Dill is an annual plant with blue-green feathery leaves, a speckled smooth stem and umbels of flat, yellow flowers. It grows easily from seed, self-sows readily but does not transplant well. The plants, which can grow to about 3 feet (1m) high, require sun and a good, light, well-drained soil with some protection from wind. They may require staking and should not be allowed to dry out.

Dill should not be confused with fennel, which has similar leaves. If in doubt, look at the stems—dill has a slender stem, fennel a bulbous one.

CULINARY USE

The chopped leaves are good added to salads and cream or cottage cheese, soups and sauces, or sprinkled over fish or meat before cooking. The flavor is clean and delicate.

The seeds can be added to sliced cucumber, beets, etc., fruit pies, meatballs and the vinegar for pickling. They can be bought, but it is nicer to use seeds that have ripened on the home-grown plant.

MEDICINAL USE

Dill-water has been used to comfort fretful, colicky babies since time immemorial.

A simple infusion of leaves and seeds has a taste babies like; nursing mothers may prefer an infusion made with wine—this will stimulate their production of milk. The infusion is also good for hiccups.

IN THE GARDEN

Dill attracts bees and repels the white cabbage moth. Planted near carrots and tomatoes, it will lure away pests but should be lifted before it flowers as, once it does, it is of no further use to the plants.

ELDER

Botanical name: *Sambucus nigra*
Family: *Caprifoliaceae*
Parts used: Bark, flowers and berries

The elder grows wild in the hedgerows of Europe and the British Isles where it makes a large bush or a small tree. The fissured bark varies in color from soft gray to mid-brown and the dark, toothed leaves have a scent as unpleasant and strong as that of the clusters of creamy flowers is light and sweet. The pretty flowers are followed by juicy black berries. Since the elder is such a useful plant, it is often introduced into the wilder parts of the garden and can be easily grown from cuttings or root divisions. Provided they have adequate sun and moisture, they seem content with any type of soil. As the roots give out a substance that aids fermentation they are good plants to use to hide the compost heap.

CULINARY USE

The berries should not be eaten raw as they have a scouring effect on the bowels, but a simple refreshing drink can be made by boiling them in water and straining when cool. A touch of lemon and honey to taste add to the flavor. They can be added to apples for a tart, used in jams and jellies and made into a syrup.

Elderberry wine is a particular country favorite. The wine made from the flowers is lighter and sharper—sometimes it is called "champagne."

ELDERFLOWER CHAMPAGNE

Ingredients

2 good handfuls elderflowers

12 pounds (700g) sugar

about 1 gallon (4L) water

1 lemon 2 tablespoonfuls white vinegar

Method

Grate the lemon rind, squeeze the juice, add to the elderflowers, sugar and vinegar. Stir. Add the water and stir again. Cover the container (preferably a large glass or china dish, or enameled saucepan—do not use an aluminum container) and leave to stand for at least 24 hours. Strain carefully, twice if necessary, and bottle, using corks well hammered in or screw tops. Leave in a dark place for at least 3 weeks before opening.

The flowers are delicate and bruise easily so should be handled lightly to avoid discoloration. The sprigs can be dipped in batter and cooked as "fritters." If the batter is kept light with the addition of a stiffly beaten egg white the muscatel taste and scent of the flowers will be retained.

The berries will store well kept in a plastic bag in the freezer but the flowers should be dried.

Elderflower vinegar is made by carefully sealing a bottle containing 22 cups (600mL) wine vinegar and 1 pound (450g) dried flowers and leaving, preferably in the sun, for 10 days. Strain the liquid several times to make as clear as possible and keep stored in the cupboard in a tightly corked or stoppered bottle. Many people who find ordinary vinegar hard on the digestion have no trouble with elderflower vinegar.

The flavor of gooseberries and elderflowers go well together. Add several clusters of the flowers to the fruit when making gooseberry jam.

ELDERBERRY SYRUP

Gently heat a quantity of washed and stalked berries in a heavy pan over low heat, mashing them to release the juice every now and again—this will take at least half an hour or so. If you have a microwave oven, heat the berries on low setting for rather less time. When the fruit is well puréed, pour into a piece of fine cloth, tie up and hang over a pan to drip overnight.

Add sugar to about a quarter-weight of the berries used, bring carefully to the boil and keep it rolling for 5 minutes. Take from the heat, skim off the scum, strain and bottle when cool.

MEDICINAL USE: Alterative, diuretic, febrifuge, sudorific.

Since the leaves and bark act quite violently on the system, they are mostly used externally.

The fresh leaves crushed and mixed with oil or butter make a good local application for the relief of piles; well stewed in water, they give a liquor which can be used to bathe away the pain of bruises, sprains, burns, scalds and sores. There was once a "magic" green ointment called Zambuck that was much used to soothe the grazes and "bad knees" of childhood.

Elderflower tea (1oz/30g flowers to 4 cups/1L water) taken hot in cupful doses will bring on the sweating which will reduce a heavy cold or prevent the onset of flu or sore throat. It will also help to clear blocked sinuses.

Syrup made from the berries, taken in hot water with honey and lemon, will serve the same purpose, as will a generous does of elderflower vinegar in hot water.

A light infusion of elderflowers (3 times the amount of fresh flowers to dried to a cup of boiling water) will, when strained and cooled, make a good compress for tired eyes. Just dip pads of cotton-wool in the infusion, squeeze out any surplus which would drip, and place the pads over the closed lids, lie down and take a rest.

COSMETIC USE

An infusion made from the flowers provides a light astringent. One teaspoonful honey mixed with a little elderflower water applied to the skin and left to dry before washing off will freshen a tired complexion.

If the skin is oily, a face mask made by mixing a few teaspoonfuls of brewers yeast into a paste with elderflower water and a little witch-hazel will correct the oiliness without unduly tightening the skin. Apply the paste to the clean skin, avoiding the eye area and leave for about half an hour before washing off with lukewarm water. Finish off with a cold rinse.

A simple and effective cream for softening and smoothing the skin is made by melting some pure lard slowly and adding stalked elderflowers, as many as the lard will take. Leave the mixture over very low heat for at least an hour—a gently burping is all that is required. Pour off and strain several times to remove all the bits and add a few drops of perfume.

HOUSEHOLD USE

Flies do not like the strong scent of elder leaves so a small branch kept in the kitchen until dry will ward them off, and a leaf rubbed over the skin while gardening will give you protection against midges.

IN THE GARDEN

Plants sprayed with a decoction made from the leaves will be given protection against biting insects.

ELECAMPNE — Scabwort, Horseheal

Botanical name: *Inula helenium*
Family: *Compositae*
Part used: Root

Elecampne, a tall perennial plant, grows wild in temperate areas. A strong plant looking rather like horseradish, it has large tapering leaves, hairy on the underside, and shaggy yellow flowers. The value of the plant is in the root and should you choose to grow it in the garden it needs a light, moist soil and sun. Propagation is best done by root division.

MEDICINAL USE: Diaphoretic, diuretic, expectorant, antiseptic.

A decoction of 1 ounce (30g) root to 22 cups (600mL) water taken in wineglassful does will help a troublesome cough and also aid digestion. It brings on perspiration and rids the body of excess water. A piece of root chewed after meals is cheaper and more effective than bought digestives. In the old days the root was candied to make a cough sweet and was thought good for asthma.

COSMETIC USE

Culpeper advised that "the distilled water of the leaves and roots together is very profitable to cleanse the skin of the face or an other parts from any morphew spots or blemishes."

EUCALYPTUS

Family: *Myrtaceae*
Part used: Oil

There are about 250 species of the family, all of which are trees. They have strong trunks, often with rough bark, and leathery grayish-greenish-whitish leaves which hang with their edges toward the sun. The leaves contain a camphorous-smelling oil.

E. globulus, E. polybractea and E. dumosa are the best-known suppliers of the famous eucalyptus oil which has been sniffed by generations of children suffering from croup and chest colds, asthma and fevers.

E. rostrata produces a red odorless gum, astringent enough to be efficient in severe cases of dysentery and diarrhea.

EVENING PRIMROSE

Botanical name: *Oenothera biennis*
Family: *Onagraceae*
Parts used: Leaves and stem

The papery, sweetly scented yellow flowers make this tall biennial a pleasant garden plant in temperate areas. It requires sun and a light, well-drained soil to enable the taproot to penetrate to a reasonable depth.

MEDICINAL USE: Astringent, sedative.

An infusion of the leaves and stems, well-strained, is useful in cases of whooping cough and asthma attacks, and is a gentle sedative.

EYEBRIGHT
Botanical name: *Euphrasia officinalis*
Family: *Scrophulariaceae*
Part used: Whole plant

This bushy little annual plant grows wild in many parts of the world and has deeply toothed, slightly hairy leaves and pinky-white lobed flowers with a yellow spot and thin red lines on the lower lobe. It grows quite well in dry places provided it has grass or other plants growing nearby from whose roots it can parasite nourishment.

MEDICINAL USE: Tonic, astringent.

The fresh juice of the plant or an infusion made from it has long been used for the disorders of the sight or local inflammation of the eyelids, such as conjunctivitis. It was said to "restore old men's sight to read small letters without spectacles that could hardly read great ones with their spectacles on." The juice or distilled water of the herb was also taken internally.

Children, slow to learn, were also said to benefit from such dosage. When the pollen count is high, eyebright tea will assist sufferers from hay fever.

FENNEL — Hinojo
Botanical name: *Foeniculum vulgare*
Family: *Umbelliferae*
Parts used: Stem, seeds, leaves and roots

Fennel grows wild in the countries around the Mediterranean Sea and has so endeared itself to man that it can be found cultivated in all parts of the world where the climate is suitable. The plant can grow to up to 7 feet (2m) in height on an erect smooth stem and has bright green feathery leaves and a handsome umbel of yellow flowers; the seeds are fissured, curved and quite large, and have a sweet taste and aroma. There are many varieties of the plant—Indian, German, Persian, Japanese, Florentine and Italian. Some are annual, others perennial. The most widely used are the last two mentioned.

Florentine fennel is an annual with a fat, swollen leaf-base; the Italian has straight, tender stems. It is easy to confuse the herb with dill—if in doubt check the seeds. Dill seeds are small and flat.

The plant is ornamental and makes a good back-of-the-border subject; it grows easily enough from seed but root division is a quicker method of increasing the stock as the seedlings do not transplant well. It needs sun but will tolerate a poorish soil provided it does not dry out too much in the heat.

CULINARY USE

The chopped leaves and stems make a refreshing addition to a salad and the chopped leaves are good in white sauce used with fish, mutton, chicken, ham and pork. Homemade cottage cheese can be given added flavor by the inclusion of some well snipped-up leaves. A little bowl of fennel seeds alongside the toothpicks will help your guests survive a rich meal without discomfort; a few chewed seeds will sweeten the breath and aid digestion. They also give a light aniseed flavor if sprinkled over plain scones before baking.

Florentine fennel can also be used as a vegetable. Cut into neat pieces, add a little salt and very little water and cook for 2-3 minutes on high in a microwave oven. You don't need much—just enough to place beside your other vegetables on the plate. Or, if the flavor is liked, cook a larger quantity as you would celery.

A dish made from fennel is popular in the south of Italy.

Sauté a quantity of cut-up stalks in olive oil and, when lightly browned but in no way scorched, add some finely chopped onion, cover with chicken stock—either fresh or made from a bought cube—and simmer until tender. Add plenty of freshly ground black pepper before serving. If liked, the dish can be topped with finely grated cheese, Parmesan for preference, and then browned under the griller.

Fennel is rich in iron, potassium, Vitamins A and C and has the added advantage of being low in kilojoules—in fact, it used to be popular as a slimming herb. A meal of boiled leaves or a handful of seeds is said to be surprisingly satisfying.

FENNEL SAUCE

A few chopped sprigs of fennel sautéed in olive oil with the addition of some tomato purée can be thickened and given a touch of mace or nutmeg for serving with fish dishes.

MEDICINAL USE: Stimulant, carminative, stomachic.

You can hardly go wrong with fennel. It is often equated with eyebright as being an herb that will preserve the eyesight. The leaves used in either infusion or decoction make an excellent eye-bath. When urination is difficult a decoction made with 1 ounce (30g) fennel root to 4 cups (1L) water and taken in wineglassful doses after meals will promote the flow very markedly. Fennel tea will increase the flow of milk in nursing mothers and generally strengthen the system; it will also relieve an acid stomach, children's colic, migraine headaches, blocked sinuses, a torpid liver or spleen, the pain of gout, rheumatism, insect bites and even snake bites. It is so excellent an herb it was once thought to have such power it would give protection against witchcraft. It certainly gives protection against fleas. Always keep a few sprigs in the dog's kennel. If you pick a bunch of fennel and squeeze it in your hand until the juices flow and then rub it into your dog's coat, he will be very pleased. Dogs love the aniseed flavor and fleas hate it. So, it was believed, do ghosts! Nervous girls regularly stuffed the keyholes with fennel seed to deny the ghosts entry.

COSMETIC USE

To fade freckles apply a mixture of warmed honey and crushed fennel seed. Leave on the skin for at least 20 minutes before washing off.

FENUGREEK — Bird's Foot

Botanical name: *Trigonella foenum-graecum*
Family: *Leguminosae*
Part used: Seeds

Fenugreek, a member of the pea and bean family, is a tallish
annual plant with trifoliate leaves, sweet-smelling yellow-cream
flowers like those of the pea, and long bean-shaped seedpods.
It will grow in most parts of the world where the heat does not
become excessive and the cold is not biting. Its use has mainly
been as a fodder crop and for the use made of the seeds as an
ingredient of curry powder, but the food value of the seeds which
contain vitamins and calcium has become increasingly recognized and the sprouted seeds, along
with those of alfalfa and the mung bean, are now used in salads, etc. The taste is not a universal
favorite, however, as it is a trifle bitter.

CULINARY USE

Mainly as a flavoring for pickles and chutney and for mixing with other spices to make curry
powder although it is sometimes used as a cake spice.

The sprouted seeds can be added to salads, cream and cottage cheese. The flavor of
fenugreek goes well with the potato. Leftover potatoes with the addition of well-chopped
fenugreek sprouts and plenty of salt and pepper can make a tasty "fry-up." Fenugreek sprouts
put in the blender with some cooked potatoes, milk and seasoning can when smooth, be heated
to make a soup.

MEDICINAL USE: Febrifuge, tonic.

Make a tonic tea by infusing ½ ounce (15g) seeds in 2½ cups (600mL) boiling water. This
tea will help the digestion, reduce fever, increase lactation, soothe the pain of tonsillitis, and
possibly, shorter the duration of a migraine.

Soak the seeds to make a poultice for boils and a softener for corns.

COSMETIC USE

The "tea" can be used as a face and hair wash.

FEVERFEW — Featherfew, Featherfoil

Botanical name: *Tanecetum parthenium*
Family: *Compositae*
Parts used: Leaves and stems

Feverfew grows wild all over Europe and turns up as a little cultivated plant in many temperate areas. The plant makes a small perennial clump and is quite pretty with slightly downy, bright green leaves which are serrated around the edges and much wider than those of its relation, Tansy (T. vulgare). The flowers are like daisies, sometimes double. The plant is quite happy growing in a dryish soil but must have sun. Propagation is easy; seed, cuttings and root division are equally successful.

MEDICINAL USE: Tonic, nervine, emmenogogic, laxative, vermifuge.

A tea made from the herb—1 ounce to ¼ cup (30g to 60mL) boiling water—is useful to quiet the nerves, promote the menses, loosen the bowels and expel worms. It is also said to be good for neuralgia.

DOMESTIC USE

The crushed leaves rubbed over the skin will keep insects at bay.

FLAX — Linseed

Botanical name: *Linum usitatissimum*
Family: *Linaceae*
Parts used: Stems and seeds

A medium-sized hardy annual, flax grows to about
20 inches (50cm) tall and has small, grayish-green leaves
and flowers of a deep, pure blue. The seeds contain
an oil which is well known to painters and housewives
and the plant fiber is used in the making of fine linen
cloth. It will grow almost anywhere given a moist, rich
soil and will self-seed readily.

CULINARY USE

Since the seeds are rich in protein, calcium and iron they can be used sprouted. Soaked
in warm water and rinsed twice a day they should, after about 4 days, have produced 2 inches
(5cm) sprouts. They are quite tasty.

MEDICINAL USE

A poultice made with the crushed seeds will reduce the inflammation of boils and swellings.

The raw seeds, once popular as a laxative, are now less so as they can sometimes irritate
the intestine, and should not be taken by expectant mothers. A cold drink made by steeping
2-3 teaspoonfuls seeds in a cup of water for a time and then straining before drinking can ease
bronchial catarrh.

HOUSEHOLD USE

Linseed oil will darken and polish wood. Mixed with turpentine it can be effective in
removing heat marks and scratches from furniture. After cane furniture has been thoroughly
washed and dried (salt water is very efficient) rub over with a drop of linseed oil on a cloth.

A mixture of equal quantities of linseed oil and turpentine with about one-third the
quantity each of vinegar and methylated spirits can be used as a furniture polish if there is
evidence of woodworm. Introduce a little of the liquid with a fine paintbrush into any hole.

FOXGLOVE — Fairy's Thimbles, Dead Men's Bells

Botanical name: *Digitalis purpurea*
Family: *Scrophulariaceae*
Part used: Leaves
Poisonous herb

Foxglove grows wild in Britain, Western Europe and New Zealand and the tall, handsome plant is often seen in cultivation. It is a biennial and will die when the seeds have ripened. The large, wrinkled, furry leaves grow in a rosette at ground level and decrease in size up the flowering stem. The tubular flowers can be deep red, purplish or white and hang their heads becomingly. The plant likes shade and can tolerate a certain amount of dryness; the fallen seed easily germinates.

This is a poisonous plant so, if you have children, think twice about including it among your garden flowers. Fortunately the leaves smell and taste nasty enough to discourage anybody from nibbling them. Curiously, foxglove is said to provide an antidote to aconite poisoning.

MEDICINAL USE: Cardiac, diuretic.

The leaves contain digitalis, which, though poisonous, is the medical drug for heart disease and high blood pressure. It acts exclusively on the heart muscles and, administered under professional supervision, can slow down, regulate and strengthen the heartbeat. No gardener should ever consider using his plants to make self-administered medicine. Digitalis will stimulate urinary function and is used in cases of suppressed urination and dropsy.

HOUSEHOLD USE

Foxglove tea, made by steeping flowers, leaves and stems in water, will prolong the life of flowers in vases.

IN THE GARDEN

Curiously, the poison of the foxglove is inactive in soil so you need have no hesitation in including pulled-up plants in the compost heap.

GARLIC

Botanical name: *Allium sativum*
Family: *Liliaceae*
Part used: Bulb

Garlic, which is thought to have originated in central Asia, has for centuries been grown all over the world. The builders of the Gizeh pyramid ate it in great quantity and the Egyptians were so impressed by its virtues they elevated the plant to the status of a god. The Hebrews, Romans, Greeks, Chinese and Indians found it both food and medicine as well as a protection against local virulent diseases

The plant is a bulb, or rather, an orb of bulblets usually called "cloves" encased in a white papery skin. The leaves are like long, flat spears, the stem is smooth and erect with tiny umbels of small white flowers growing at the apex. The whole plant has a strong, lingering odor—it cannot be called scent or aroma due to the essential oil it contains. This oil is antibiotic and contains Vitamins A and B, sulfur and iodine. Garlic grows easily given sun, adequate moisture and a light, well-drained but not impoverished soil. The cloves can be planted in drills, like onions, and should be kept free from weeds. When the leaves start to turn brown at the beginning of autumn the plant can be dug up and hung to dry, or the cloves can be separated and replanted.

CULINARY USE

The cardinal rule with garlic is: never too much. A rub around the salad bowl with a bruised clove or over meat before cooking can be quite enough for many people; on the other hand there are garlic addicts who love the heavy pungent flavor and do not care that it hangs on the breath. If you cook for them do a general kindness by providing sprigs of parsley for them to chew when the meal is finished—just cleaning the teeth will do no good at all.

Another way to achieve a light taste of garlic is to cook food in oil in which peeled garlic cloves have been standing for a few days. If you soak the cloves in water for a few hours before using them you will reduce the smell but not the taste.

Meat, fish, vegetables, salads, soups and stews can all benefit from the judicious addition of a little crushed garlic and, of course, there is the popular garlic bread.

GARLIC BREAD

Crush 2 cloves garlic and add to 4½ ounces (125g) soft butter. Add salt and pepper. Cut a loaf of French bread in diagonal slices from the top, stopping short of making a cut through the bottom. Spread the garlic butter on each side of the slices thickly, close up the loaf and wrap in aluminum foil. You can either heat the loaf in a fairly sharp oven or over the barbecue.

Instead of providing *croutons* of plain bread for soups try bread spread on each side with garlic butter and then bake until golden and crisp.

GARLIC SAUCE

This is a wonderful sauce to keep in the refrigerator for use with a plain vegetable.

Ingredients

4 garlic cloves

1 teaspoon mustard powder

2 egg yolks

2 cup (165mL) olive oil

lemon sauce

seasoning

Method

Crush the garlic cloves by hammering well and remove the papery skin. Beat the egg yolks, add salt, pepper, mustard powder, garlic and mix well. Add the oil slowly and carefully, whisking all the time, and when the mixture is thick add the lemon juice and whisk again.

For a strong-tasting but truly delicious and different soup, try this one.

GARLIC SOUP

Sauté 2 heaped tablespoonfuls finely chopped garlic in olive oil. Add at least 12 ounces (350g) brown breadcrumbs (they can be quite coarse) and stir over the heat until the mixture becomes pleasantly brown. Add 4 cups (1L) of chicken stock (can be made from bought cubes) and simmer for at least half an hour.

Put the mixture through a blender until smooth. Return to a saucepan and over very low heat add 2 or 3 well-beaten eggs, some salt and a generous amount of freshly ground black pepper. If you like a hotter taste, use cayenne pepper instead. Gently and carefully bring the soup to simmering point but on no account allow it to boil or the eggs will toughen. Pour into serving bowls and give each one a light dusting of paprika.

MEDICINAL USE: Antiseptic, diaphoretic, diuretic, expectorant, stomachic, vermifuge, carminative, antispasmodic.

Garlic juice is a useful first-aid antiseptic. Just press a cut bulb against any wound or on a boil that will not come to a head or over troublesome pimples. "With Figge leaves and Cumin it is laid on against the Bitings of the Mouse," the well-respected Gerard said. The crushed cloves make a good poultice for painful sores slow to heal and rubbed on a corn regularly will loosen it. The antiseptic qualities are also useful internally and will ward off infectious diseases and the proliferation of harmful bacteria in stomach and intestines. Garlic juice made into a syrup with honey will ease coughs, colds and asthma, and helps to move the mucus of bronchitis and catarrh. A hot drink made by pouring boiling water or milk over a few crushed cloves will ease stomachic upset. Taken regularly it will help to keep a high blood pressure within reasonable limits and work against arteriosclerosis. Garlic "perles" can be bought commercially and many people attribute their continuing good health to taking a dose each morning with the first cup of tea. These "perles" have no noticeable odor. A simple and effective rub for a tight chest can be made by chopping up a whole head of garlic and stirring it into a small jar of plain vaseline. After about a week in a warm place the essential oil will have incorporated with the vaseline and can be rubbed on the chest. Smelly, but it works well.

IN THE GARDEN

Clumps of garlic planted near rose bushes will help to keep them free of aphids. Planted beneath apple trees they will protect them against scab, under peach trees against leaf curl, and near tomatoes against red spiders.

Mosquitoes dislike the whiff of garlic so pots near the outdoor eating area in the garden are very useful.

A spray made by soaking 4 crushed cloves of garlic in 4 cups (1L) of water for several days will kill ants, spiders, caterpillars, the cabbage worm and the tomato worm.

GENTIAN—Yellow Gentian

Botanical name: *Gentiana lutea*
Family: *Gentianaceae*
Parts used: Root and leaves

There are many different species of gentian but the yellow gentian is the most usual one used medicinally. *Gentiana kochiana*, the blue-flowered type, also has medicinal properties.

The yellow variety is a perennial plant which grows about 3 feet (1m) high and although slow to flower can live a very long time indeed. The shiny 5-veined leaves grow opposite each other on the tall stem and the deep yellow, many-stemmed flowers grow from the leaf axils. The root, which is the important part of the plant, is thick and fleshy and can grow to almost 3 feet (1m) in length.

Since it takes so long to flower—some people say 10 years—it is not a popular garden plant although it is so handsome. If you want to try it, grow from root cuttings. Its natural habitat is the mountainous areas of Europe so it would clearly be useless to attempt to grow it in a warm climate.

MEDICINAL USE: Tonic, stomachic, anthelmintic, antiseptic.

The young bruised leaves make a good poultice for inflamed wounds but, although the root makes such an excellent tonic, it is wise to take any gentian preparation under medical supervision and it should never be taken by pregnant women or anyone suffering from high blood pressure as it has such a pronounced effect on the blood. Its powerful tonic properties have been recognized for over 2,000 years and its action on the body is rather like that of quinine. It is good for poor circulation, anemia, impure blood, weak digestion, suppressed menstruation and urine, chills, fevers, liver and spleen complaints, insect and snakebites and the expulsion of worms from the body.

GERANIUM
Botanical name: *Pelargonium*
Family: *Geraniaceae*
Part used: Leaves

Every garden should have at least a few of the scented-leaved geraniums because, although their culinary use is fairly limited, the dried leaves are an invaluable addition to potpourri, scented sachets and herb pillows.

There are many different varieties—the scent of the leaves ranges through apple, almond, apricot, coconut, lemon, nutmeg, peppermint, orange, lime and rose, to name the best known. Geranium specialists could probably suggest even more.

Few people have the patience to grow geraniums from seed—stem cuttings are the quickest and easiest method. If you buy one plant you can happily propagate from that but often one plant of a variety is adequate for most needs. Since the flowers are insignificant compared to the unscented types, the plants are often confined to the herb garden or grown in pots that can be moved around. The rose-scented geranium (*P. graveolens*) makes a fine bushy plant up to 3 feet (1m) in height and quite wide, and is very pleasant to have growing where the leaves are brushed in passing and the scent released.

CULINARY USE

One or two fresh leaves added to cakes, jellies and puddings or stewed fruit give a clean and unusual flavor. A plain egg custard, which is often dusted with powdered nutmeg, will have the same flavor if the leaves of the nutmeg-scented type are used instead.

The chopped leaves can be added to cottage cheese and plain yogurt. Try a light sprinkling over a fresh fruit salad or to improve the taste of an herbal tea.

The leaves can be used dried but the appearance is not as pleasant.

GERANIUM JELLY

You could use any of the flavored leaves depending on preference, though the general favorite seems to be the rose-geranium.

Cut up a quantity of sharp green apples retaining the skin and pips and add a good handful of leaves, well washed. Cover with water and cook in a heavy pan by bringing to a slow boil and then keeping at simmering point for at least half an hour. Take from the heat and allow to cool a little before pouring into a bag made of fine cloth which can be suspended over a pan. You could up-end a stool and tie a square of muslin to each leg, place a pan beneath it and then pour the purée onto the muslin. Leave to drib overnight.

Measure the juice, add 1 pound (450g) granulated sugar to each 2½ cups (600mL) juice and heat slowly in a heavy pan until the sugar is dissolved, stirring every now and then. Bring to the boil carefully and watch as it boils for about 10 minutes.

Remove scum. When sufficiently cooled, pour into clean warm jars, keeping the skin, which will form as the jelly cools slightly, to one side. Do not leave an air gap any larger than strictly necessary at the top of each jar. Cover each one with a circle of waxed paper and leave until cold before sealing the jars.

COSMETIC USE

You can buy rose-geranium oil to add to your bath water or you could pour boiling water over a handful of crushed leaves and let it stand for a while, strain and then add to your bath.

The old practice of restoring balance to a skin made tight and uncomfortable by the frequent use of soap was to gently dab it over with cotton-wool soaked in a weak solution of vinegar and water, but many people do not like the vinegar smell. Try a vinegar made by leaving crushed geranium leaves in a bottle of white or cider vinegar. If you leave the bottle in the sun for a few weeks and then strain it well you will find the vinegar smell will disappear leaving the scent of the leaves. Any cosmetic vinegar should be used diluted. Use at least 7 times as much water as vinegar.

The medicinal use is slight but the leaves do have antiseptic properties and if you have nothing else on hand a poultice made from the bruised leaves will come in handy for a cut or bad graze.

IN THE GARDEN

Grown near a vine geraniums can repel the Japanese beetle, which can be such a dread-ful nuisance and half ruin the crop.

GERMANDER

Botanical name: *Teucrium*
Family: *Labiatae*
Part used: Whole plant

Germander grows wild in Europe and Britain where it was once a popular medicinal herb. Today it is mostly used as a decorative garden plant in all temperate parts of the world. There are several different varieties ranging from the prostrate to the tall and bushy, and they all have attractive leaves and flowers.

The pointed, oval, shiny leaves and pink flowers of Wall Germander (*Teucrium chamaedrys*) make an attractive border edging or low hedge and the prostrate variety an excellent ground cover. The sage-leaved variety (*T. scorodonia*) has greenish-yellow flowers and wrinkled leaves, which smell rather like beer.

In their native state germanders grow in acid soil in the shade but are quite good-tempered in the garden provided the soil does not become soggy.

MEDICINAL USE: Stimulant, tonic, diaphoretic, diuretic.

Culpeper said that the liquid extract of Wall Germander "strengthens the brain and apprehension exceedingly and relieves them when drooping" so it is hard to see why it is so little used today. Tea made from the sage-leaved variety will cleanse the blood and rid the body of excess water, promote menstruation, reduce fever and generally tone up the system.

GINGER
Botanical name: *Zingiber officinale*
Family: *Zingiberaceae*
Part used: Root (rhizome)

Ginger is a perennial plant native to tropical South-East Asia and is widely cultivated in other tropical parts of the world. Jamaican ginger is considered to be the best of all. The plant grows from large creeping rhizomes that put up bright green, broad, flat, tapering leaves. The flowers are yellow or white with purple lips. The fat, knobbly rhizomes are the part of the plant valuable to man. Ginger root can be bought fresh, dried, ground, candied, or in syrup, and it has wide culinary and medicinal values.

In its native state ginger requires a hot climate with the humidity given by heavy rainfall but it is possible to grow it in a pot in cooler areas if adequate water is provided and winter protection given but, since the root is so readily available commercially, few people consider it a worthwhile enterprise. Should you wish to try, set a piece of bought ginger root just below the surface of the soil (which should be rich and well drained) in a large pot, and when the leaves begin to show, water well. As growth increases keep the leaves lightly sprayed to encourage humidity. You can winter the plant in a greenhouse where it will become dormant and then revive with the warmer weather but, since young roots have the best flavor, you could discard the plant at the end of the first year and use the root, keeping a portion aside for replanting for a new crop. In the States of New South Wales and Queensland in Australia, a plant of the family Alpinia coerulea is known as Native Ginger. It grows tall and erect, 5-62 feet (1.5-2m), and has large pale-green leaves, white and red flowers and can make a good shade plant in moist rich soil. Only the root-tips have the strong flavor of ginger. Other varieties (A. arctiflora and A. arundelliana) make striking indoor plants for large buildings that have constant, even heat.

CULINARY USE

Ginger root has a sweet, hot flavor, which goes with meat, fish, vegetables, cakes and sweets. There must be very few people who do not like the taste. It can be bought green, i.e. fresh, for use with savory foods and is often used in Chinese cooking. If you find a recipe that specifies fresh ginger and have only the ground variety on hand you can use that instead but only use quarter the amount suggested.

The Chinese pickle ginger by scraping the root and then cutting it into very thin, small slices which are covered with salt and left for about an hour and a half. When it is rinsed and drained it is boiled in a strong solution of sugar and white vinegar for a minute or two and then sealed in sterilized jars. Preserved ginger is widely sold in attractive little Oriental pots but you can easily preserve your own.

PRESERVED GINGER

Scrape the roots clean and cut into small pieces about 2 inch (1cm) square and leave to stand in cold water for at least an hour, preferably longer. Drain and bring to the boil in just enough water to cover the pieces and hold at the boil for 5-6 minutes. Drain. Re-cover with water, bring to the boil and then keep at simmering point until the ginger is tender.

Make a syrup using twice as much sugar as water, simmering very carefully, then add the drained ginger. Bring back to the boil and simmer for about 10 minutes. Leave to stand for 24 hours, preferably removing to a glass container.

The next day strain off the syrup and add more sugar and simmer over low heat until all sugar is dissolved. Pour over the drained ginger and leave to stand for another 24 hours. Strain again, add more sugar to the syrup and repeat the previous day's process. When all the sugar has dissolved and the syrup has simmered for a few minutes, pour it over the ginger and when cool enough pour into warm sterilized jars. The syrup is obviously very sweet. The ginger can be removed from the syrup and dried very slowly in a very low oven to give crystallized ginger.

A simple tasty drink can be made using only a small piece of fresh ginger root.

GINGER DRINK

Ingredients

⅔ ounce (20g) ginger root, well bruised
1 ounce (30g) fresh yeast
1 ounce (30g) cream of tartar
1 pound (450g) sugar
juice of 1 lemon, with finely grated rind
5 pints (2.5L) boiling water

Method

Put the ginger, sugar, cream of tartar and grated lemon rind in a big jug that will withstand boiling water. Pour on the water and leave to stand until cool. Mix yeast and lemon juice with a little cold water until smooth and then add to the mixture and stir in. Leave to stand, covered, for 12 hours. Pour into screw-top bottles—you can use corked ones—and leave somewhere cool and dark for the next 2 days. Open carefully.

Gingerbread, ginger biscuits and gingerbread men are all-time favorites which are made using the powdered root, but the preserved ginger can be added to cakes, puddings, stewed fruit and chutneys equally well. For an exotic after-dinner drink to surprise your guests, try coffee made with the addition of some ground ginger. This will, of course, be served in very small cups. The amounts for 4 people are: 1 cup cold water to 6 teaspoons powdered coffee, 6 teaspoons of sugar and 2 teaspoons of ground ginger. Mix all the ingredients together and carefully bring to the boil. Take off the heat and let the liquid become still. Then put on the heat and boil up again, etc. Repeat the boiling up, allow to settle 3 times in all and then serve. Since the process is very like the one used for making Turkish coffee you could make it in one of those attractive long-handled, tapered pots.

MEDICINAL USE: Stimulant, carminative, expectorant.

Powdered ginger with sugar to taste in hot water makes a warming drink f[...]
the cold, having a cold, suffering from stomachic wind and spasms, or retention of urine. It
is often used with other herbs to release phlegm that has gathered on the chest, and since it
contains sulfur it will help to rid the blood of impurities. During "plague" years of earlier times
it was considered a valuable antidote. Putting 2 tablespoonfuls ground ginger in the bath will
bring on healing perspiration. Whisky kept for warming or medicinal purposes can be improved
by adding a small piece of bruised ginger root, a handful of raisins, a good cup of sugar, the
juice of a lemon and 2-3 teaspoons caraway seeds per bottle. Put it all in a wide-necked jar which
can be corked or screwed down and hide in a cupboard for a fortnight, visiting it daily to give it
a good shake. Strain and bottle. You will, no doubt, think of something to do with the raisins.

GINSENG
Botanical name: *Panax*
Family: *Araliaceae*
Part used: Root

The generic name Panax means "all-healing,"
like panacea, and gives a good idea of how the
early botanists thought of it.

P. *schinseng* is the variety which grows in
China and P. *quinquefolium* the one which grows
in North America.

The plants reach less than 30 inches (75cm) high, have 5-lobed leaves, greenish-white flowers
which grow in an umbel, red berries and a largish tap-root. This is the "magic root" which makes
the most famous of all Chinese medicines and is reputed to give long life, health and happiness.
So much of it is used in China that the cultivated American variety has to be imported.

MEDICINAL USE: Demulcent, stomachic, tonic, stimulant, febrifuge.

Ginseng root will promote appetite, stimulate the central nervous system and so relieve weariness that sometimes it can be a gentle aphrodisiac. It eases an upset stomach and an inflamed bladder, is good for constipation; taken hot it will bring on sweating which will break a cold and ease a cough. It can reduce the level of choles¬terol and thereby bring down blood pressure. The Chinese take it regularly, believing it will give protection against any disease.

Anyone exhausted by prolonged emotional or mental strain would lose nothing and might gain a lot by starting to take ginseng regularly. There are an awful lot of Chinese and they have been taking this medicine, with enthusiasm, for a very long time and they are a highly pragmatic race.

GOLDEN ROD
Botanical name: *Solidago virgaurea*
Family: *Compositae*
Parts used: Flowering tips and leaves

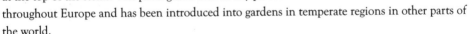

In English gardens the flowering of golden rod heralds the ending of summer. The tall perennial plant grows at least 3 feet (1m) high with a rather angular stem, narrow tapering leaves and golden-yellow flowers growing in loosely-branched clusters at the top of the stems. The plant grows wild in dry places throughout Europe and has been introduced into gardens in temperate regions in other parts of the world.

MEDICINAL USE: Carminative, stimulant, astringent, diuretic, vulnerary.

The crushed leaves can be applied directly to a wound, or an infusion made from fresh or dried flower-tips and leaves can be used for bathing cuts, etc. It will disinfect, staunch bleeding and draw the tissues together. The same infusion, made by pouring 2½ cups (600mL) boiling water over 1 ounce (30g) of the dried plant and taken in wineglassful doses several times a day, will stimulate the action of the liver and kidneys and rid the body of accumulated poisons and unwanted water, ease any inflammation of the digestive organs and the genito-urinary region and, by a general cleansing of the body, aid sufferers from rheumatic and arthritic pain and spotty complexions. It is one of the best cleansing herbs known and has even been credited with the ability to break up kidney stones.

GOLDEN SEAL — Orange Root, Yellow Root

Botanical name: *Hydrastis canadensis*
Family: *Ranunculaceae*
Part used: Root

This perennial plant was well known to the Indians of North America and the early settlers but it is now uncommon in the wild and has to be cultivated. It needs moisture and shade for the low-growing plant with its few deeply-cut, wrinkled, hairy leaves and pale, many-stamened flowers and strange, bright yellow root to survive, let alone to grow well, but the effort is worthwhile for it is one of the finest medicinal plants in the herbal kingdom.

MEDICINAL USE: Alterative, antiperiodic, antiseptic, aperient, diuretic, de-obstruent, detergent, ophthalmic, tonic.

Bought preparations of golden seal are good for: allergies, asthma, bleeding (external and internal), bowel and bladder problems, bronchitis, burns, colds, colitis, constipation, diabetes, digestive upset, eye affections, hay fever and sinus trouble, infectious fevers, kidney, liver and spleen disorders, skin disorders such as psoriasis and eczema, syphilis, tonsillitis, ulcers, vaginal discharge, and voice loss. The list of conditions for which it can be used is one of the most impressive of all the medicinal herbs but, since the plant cannot be widely grown and gardeners are unlikely to have success even if they try, this is one case where reliance on commercial production is almost total.

GOOSEGRASS

Botanical name: *Galium aparine*
Family: *Rubiaceae*
Part used: Whole plant

Goosegrass is such a pest as a weed in temperate climates it is good to know it can show another face and be of good use. This annual plant has soft long stems, small, pointed, bristly leaves, tiny white flowers which produce small prickly seeds which, like the leaves, catch in anything and everything within their orbit.

CULINARY USE

You can at least try, once, the young leaves and tops of a good weeding of goosegrass as a vegetable or chopped and added to soup. The taste is not remarkable but it is not unpleasant either and you will have had a cheap and easy intake of vitamins and silica. I once read somewhere that the dried seeds can be roasted and ground to make a coffee-type drink. No mention was made of the amount of seeds needed and they are very small.

MEDICINAL USE: Antiseptic, tonic.

Goosegrass is another of the herbs whose leaves can be used as instant first-aid. A handful made into a poultice will relieve the pain of sores and grazes, and a tea made by pouring boiling water over the plant and leaving until reasonably cool makes an excellent sunburn lotion and good hair tonic. Goosegrass is both cleanser and soother. Acting as a laxative which does not purge, it will clear the skin and, by ridding the blood of impurities, will strengthen the system— as a soother it will help the insomniac.

The only warning is that since it increases blood sugar it should not be taken internally by diabetics.

GROUND ELDER — Goutweed, Bishops Elder, Herb Gerard

Botanical name: *Aegopodium podragria*
Parts used: Leaves and root

People who have ground elder in their garden commiserate with each other as fellow-sufferers from a dreadful disease; this is a very difficult weed to eradicate. The root system is formidable; it spreads and chokes other plants growing nearby. It is not the prettiest of weeds either, although the large toothed leaves do have a "not unpleasant" scent and the umbels of white flowers have an insignificant daintiness. It is a surprise to find that it was once actually cultivated, not only for its culinary use but also for its medicinal value.

CULINARY USE

Young leaves lightly cooked with butter and lemon juice will be acceptable to all who like spinach.

MEDICINAL USE

A gentle sedative can be made by infusing fresh or dried leaves in boiling water. You will need at least 3 times the amount of fresh leaves to dried.

A poultice made from the boiled roots and leaves will relieve the pain of rheumatism or gout.

GROUND IVY — Creeping Jenny, Alehoof, Haymaids, Gill-go-over-ground

Botanical name: *Glechoma bederacea*
Family: *Labiatae*
Part used: Leaves

Ground ivy grows wild in many parts of the world. The perennial evergreen is a great ground-cover, with kidney-shaped, dark-green leaves, scalloped round the edges and bluish-purple, 2-

lipped flowers growing in the axils of the leaves at the top of the stems. It is attractive but if you plant it in your garden, keep it well-curbed or it will take over.

MEDICINAL USE: Astringent, diuretic, tonic.

A tea made from the leaves, 1 ounce (30g) to 2½ cups (600mL) boiling water, will help the digestion, aid the action of the kidneys, bring on menstruation and ease a troublesome cough. It makes a good tonic for the anemic. Like most herbal teas, it is more palatable if sweetened with a little honey. Country people used to use a poultice made of ground elder leaves and yarrow and chamomile flowers for bringing stubborn abscesses and boils to bursting point.

GROUNDSEL
Botanical name: *Senecio vulgaris*
Family: *Compositae*
Parts used: Leaves and stems

Groundsel is a common weed, which grows in gardens all over the world and stays in flower for many months. Low-growing and quick-spreading, it has small yellow flowers. Caged birds, particularly canaries, love it.

MEDICINAL USE: Diuretic, diaphoretic.

A weak groundsel tea will relieve biliousness, a strong one will act as a purgative. An old-fashioned but well-proven remedy for the pain and stress of an irregular menstrual cycle is a decoction of 1w ounce (50g) fresh groundsel to 4 cups (1L) of water.

A dry chapped skin will benefit from bathing in a simple groundsel "tea."

HAWTHORN — May, Whitethorn, Bird Eagles

Botanical name: *Crataegus oxycantha*
Family: *Rosaceae*
Parts used: Leaf-buds, flowers and berries

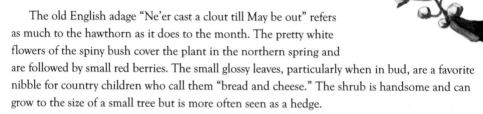

The old English adage "Ne'er cast a clout till May be out" refers as much to the hawthorn as it does to the month. The pretty white flowers of the spiny bush cover the plant in the northern spring and are followed by small red berries. The small glossy leaves, particularly when in bud, are a favorite nibble for country children who call them "bread and cheese." The shrub is handsome and can grow to the size of a small tree but is more often seen as a hedge.

CULINARY USE

The leaf-buds, which are pleasantly flavored, can be eaten alone or added to a salad. The red berries can be made into a jelly that goes well with cold meats.

MEDICINAL USE: Cardiac, tonic, sedative, diuretic, antispasmodic.

Hawthorn has properties that make it a strong cardiac tonic and even a remedy for organic and functional disorders of the heart. It will regulate blood pressure whether high or low and since it is non-toxic can be taken for a long period, unlike other drugs, which build up in the system with unpleasant effect.

A simple infusion of flowers in boiling water can be taken regularly and a cup taken at bedtime will help to ensure a good night's sleep. It is said that if an infusion is taken as soon as the first symptoms of angina appear there is a very good chance the condition will not develop any further.

The dried berries, which share the properties of the leaves and flowers are usually used in decoction for loose bowels or as a gargle for a sore throat—or an infusion of 3 teaspoons dried berries to 1 cup boiling water left to stand until cool and then reheated.

Hawthorn is often prescribed in conjunction with Cactus grandiflora. Garlic and green pepper also make a good combination.

COSMETIC USE

A decoction of the flowers and berries makes a good face-wash for acne sufferers.

HEMLOCK

Botanical name: *Conium maculatum*
Family: *Umbelliferae*
Poisonous plant

All that most people know about hemlock is that Socrates died from a dose of it.

The plant is certainly poisonous, but in common with other poisonous plants has beneficial usage. The biennial plant grows wild in temperate Europe and since it looks so like other members of the *Umbelliferae* family, such as carrot, fennel and, to a lesser extent, parsley, it is probably best avoided—something which it is easy to do since it gives off the stuffy, nasty smell of mice droppings.

It is an attractive enough plant with purple-blotched, smooth hollow stems, graceful, feathery leaves and umbels of white flowers just like those of fool's parsley—or cow parsley, if you like. Since it will grow in any temperate climate always check any plants of the family you pick in the wild.

The narcotic drug the plant contains is extracted and used in commercial preparations as a sedative and antispasmodic but is use is very much less than it used to be.

HENBANE

Botanical name: *Hyoscyamus niger*
Family: *Solanaceae*
Parts used: Leaves and flower tops

The flowers of henbane are attractive—a dusky yellow with delicate purple tracery but the gray-green leaves are sticky, hairy and smelly and if you find the plant growing wild near your hen-yard, grub it up at once or you will lose your chicks.

Dr. Crippen was aware of the power of henbane and used it to get rid of his wife. The plant can be recognized even when the flowers have gone because the seedpods that replace them look like a jaw of teeth.

The leaves and flowering tops contain the alkaloid drug hyoscyamine, which is sedative, narcotic and antispasmodic, and used in preparations administered under professional advice for the treatment of nervous disorders and whooping cough.

HOPS
Botanical name: *Humulus lupulus*
Family: *Cannabinaceae*
Parts used: Buds, young leaves, young tips and dried flower-cones

Hops are cultivated in many countries for use in the manufacture of beer and the hop-fields of Kent in the south of England are renowned for the superior quality of their crops. The plant is a perennial climber of great vigor, with squarish, thick stems and pale-green, rough, dentate leaves like that of the vine.

The female flowers are small and round and become cone-shaped as they mature; the male flowers hang in loose clusters. There are male and female plants and though only the female flower-cones are used, male plants are found in the hopfields as the fertilized cones grow more rapidly and become larger than unfertilized ones.

A few female plants make a pleasant addition to the garden and can be propagated quite easily from cuttings. Given an open rich soil and plenty of sun and water they will make a clockwise ascent of any trellis, pergola or wires provided, and may have to be restrained from smothering small shrubs etc. Since the plant is perennial it can be cut down when the cones are ripe enough for drying—you will probably have just enough to make into a fragrant herb pillow the scent from which will ease the nerves and give restful sleep.

CULINARY USE

The young shoots can be cooked as for asparagus tips, and if the new buds and leaves are blanched to get rid of the bitter taste, they too can be used as a vegetable.

The dried female cones are, of course, used to give beer its flavor and add to its keeping quality.

MEDICINAL USE: Anodyne, aromatic bitter, diuretic, tonic, sedative.

Tea made from the dried cones aids the digestion, stimulates the appetite and calms the nerves, relieves menstrual pain and cramps, purifies the blood and gives insomniacs the chance of a restful night's sleep. It also has a soothing effect on the male sexual responses, reducing the pressures and thereby relieving the pain of constant erection and too frequent involuntary emission of semen. A decoction made by boiling up 1¾ ounce (50g) dried hops in 4 cups (1L) of water and keeping at the boil for about 3 minutes before allowing to cool sufficiently to drink, should be taken in cupful doses 3 times a day for the last-mentioned condition.

HOREHOUND — White Horehound

Botanical name: *Marrubium vulgare*
Family: *Labiateae*
Part used: Leaves

The sprawling habit of horehound can make it a tiresome garden plant and the green and white wrinkled, hairy leaves and small white flowers are less than handsome, nevertheless it is good-tempered enough to tolerate spots in which other plants would refuse to thrive and makes a splendid edging, albeit with a tendency to die off if the winter cold becomes too sharp.

Horehound leaves, which taste rather like a bitter thyme, make splendid beer; honey made where bees have access to horehound blossom has a beautiful flavor and a cough candy that is decidedly moreish and a good warming tea can be made from the leafy tops, so horehound should not be considered lightly. Black horehound—Ballota nigra—is something different. The leaves are very similar to those of the white horehound but the flowers are purple and the whole plant stinks so badly that no animal in its native Europe will eat it.

The Greeks, with great good sense, saw how useful it might be against rabies, and even today composite antispasmodic medicines often contain black horehound. Since violent convulsions are one of the symptoms of rabies the years have clearly proved the Greeks were right. White horehound is quite different in its beneficial action.

CULINARY USE

HOREHOUND BEER

Ingredients

2 ounces (60g) leaves and stems, well chopped

1 ounce (30g) fresh ginger root, heavily bruised

Juice 1 lemon

2 good pinches tartaric acid

1 pound (450g) brown sugar

2 tablespoons fresh yeast

1 teaspoon molasses

Method

Cover leaves and ginger with water and gently bring to the boil in a large heavy pan over controlled heat. Maintain at a steady rolling boil for about half-an-hour, occasionally pressing the contents against the side of the saucepan with a wooden spoon to help extract the goodness.

Take from the heat and add the sugar and enough boiling water to bring the liquid content up to about 1 gallon (4L); stir until the sugar is wholly dissolved. Leave to stand for about 15 minutes then add lemon juice, tartaric acid and molasses, stir well. When liquid is gently cool, add the fresh yeast, well crumbled. After a few minutes strain the liquid (some people do it twice) into bottles and leave in a dark place for 2-3 days before corking. The beer will be ready in just over a fortnight. Do not expose the bottles to the light until ready to use. A longer, possibly simpler but certainly more tedious, method is to boil up a great handful of chopped leaves and stems in about 22 gallons (10L) of water to which about 2 pounds (900g) black treacle or molasses have been added. Keep the mixture at a rolling boil for at least an hour—this requires attention as imagine the mess if it all boiled over. Take off the heat and allow to stand until cool enough to strain without danger of scalding oneself. Add 2 tablespoons fresh well-crumbled yeast and leave to stand, protected by a cloth, for a whole day. Bottle. The beer will be ready in a week to 10 days.

HOREHOUND TOFFEE

This makes a good cough candy.

Ingredients

1 ounce (30g) dried horehound leaves
or 2-3 ounces (60-90g) fresh leaves
Boiling water

Sugar
Tartaric acid

Method

Pour 4 cups (1L) boiling water over the horehound and leave it to stand for an hour. Strain well—get all the bits of dried horehound leaves out; fresh ones can be lifted out with a perforated spoon—in any case make sure the remaining liquid is good and clear. Add ¾ pound (360g) sugar (brown of course) and 1 teaspoon cream of tartar for every cup of liquid.

Stir well, pour into a heavy pan and carefully bring to the boil and hold it there until small spoonfuls of the mixture dropped into cold water become hard—the classic "toffee-test"! Butter a shallow pan and pour the candy into it. When wrinkles show the toffee is beginning to set, mark out into squares with a knife dipped in water.

Leave until hard and then strike the underneath of the tin with a few sharp blows to dislodge and break up the toffee into squares which should be immediately transferred to an airtight tin or jar.

MEDICINAL USE: Tonic, expectorant, diuretic, laxative, vermifuge.

The plant contains not only iron and potassium but the drug marrubin which stimulates the appetite and the action of the liver and enables sufferers to cough up troublesome phlegm. If you suffer from the "wheezes," suck horehound toffee, drink horehound beer or at least drink horehound tea made by pouring 2½ cups (600mL) boiling water over 1 ounce (30g) dried horehound leaves. Honey makes a good sweetener. Just as horehound enables the body to get rid of chest mucus, it enables it to expel afterbirth and worms. Since it helps the body to get rid of excess water it is also a weight-reducer—make it strong for this, but be prepared for its laxative properties.

Together with coltsfoot leaves, horehound is used in some herbal tobaccos.

HOUSEHOLD USE

Flies do not like its scent so keep some in the kitchen and pantry, tuck some in the band of your gardening hat and keep a bunch steeping in a bowl of water for a splash over face and arms before venturing out on one of "those" days.

HORSERADISH

Botanical name: *Amoracia rusticana*
Family: *Cruciferae*
Part used: Root

Call it "Cochlearia amoracia" if you wish—we will both be referring to the same plant: a tall perennial, native to the mud of Eastern Europe, with large, lance-shaped leaves, sometimes notched, small 4-petalled white flowers and a thick tapering root rather like the parsnip, with a flavor pungent enough to make the eyes water.

Its remarkable properties were so appreciated that horseradish's popularity spread far beyond its origins and today it is cultivated in many parts of the world and can be found growing wild too, for it is a great "escaper," which is curious because the seeds in the round pods are notoriously unwilling to ripen unless conditions are just right. Propagation of your cultivated plants should be done by chopping the root into sections, or even slivers. When introducing horseradish into the garden, give it a cool moist spot in well-drained deeply-dug soil because the root strikes deep, and plant with the tops of the sections about 1 inch (2.5cm) beneath the soil. Planted near the potato bed or fruit trees, horseradish will provide welcome protection against fungus and if you chop up the leaves finely and make into a "tea," you have a useful spray to use when fruit trees show actual signs of monilia. If you dig up the plant in order to dry the roots, make certain you get all the "bits" for any root particle left is almost certain to produce another plant—two or at the most three horseradish plants are enough to cope with the culinary and medicinal needs of any normal-sized family.

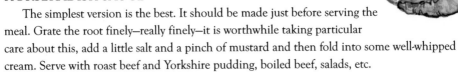

CULINARY USE

HORSERADISH SAUCE

The simplest version is the best. It should be made just before serving the meal. Grate the root finely—really finely—it is worthwhile taking particular care about this, add a little salt and a pinch of mustard and then fold into some well-whipped cream. Serve with roast beef and Yorkshire pudding, boiled beef, salads, etc.

For weight-watchers yogurt can be substituted for the cream and a splash of cider vinegar added. Don't be tempted to cook horseradish—for some reason cooking destroys the flavor and if you do not have fresh horseradish, buy the dehydrated commercial type which can be reconstituted by soaking the dried flakes in water.

Personally I feel horseradish is better forgotten unless you can make your own preparation from the fresh root.

A savory butter can be made by pounding grated horseradish into butter and then pressing the mixture through a fine sieve. If you are a particularly good pounder, the sieving will not be necessary. Again this should be used almost at once.

MEDICINAL USE: Stimulant, diaphoretic, diuretic.

Legend has it that horseradish was one of the bitter herbs eaten at the Passover. Coriander, horehound, lettuce and nettles were the other four. Somehow imagination falters as to how they were served. The high Vitamin C content and the way horseradish can kill harmful bacteria in the intestinal tract make the plant doubly useful; it also stimulates digestion and rids the system of excessive water. Wineglassful doses, three times a day, of 22 cups (600mL) boiling water poured over 1 ounce (30g) well-hammered horseradish root is recommended.

When you think of the way horseradish sauce can make the eyes water, it is no surprise to find that the root, fresh or powdered, can clear clogged sinuses.

To rid the body of mucous waste, eat horseradish. Fine-grating is always the answer. Try a brown bread sandwich of it, with plenty of butter and a touch of tarragon or dill. Sneak a little grated horseradish into cooked vegetable and meat dishes, homemade cheeses, mayonnaises etc. Mix fresh-boiled grated beet with grated horseradish, well seasoned in sweetened vinegar to make a thick relish for use with fish or meat dishes. All the culinary uses of horseradish can be thought of as being medicinal too.

IN THE GARDEN

Young horseradish leaves made into a tea can be used as a spray for fruit trees showing signs of monilia.

HORSETAIL

Botanical name: *Equisetum arvense*
Family: *Equisitaceae*
Part used: Whole plant

It is hard to believe that the unprepossessing horsetail can be such a splendidly generous plant with such a wide variety of uses. What other plant will enrich the blood, remove white spots on fingernails and clean dirty saucepans?

The tough stems, crowned with heads that look a bit like miniature asparagus, rise from a rhizomatous and fast-creeping root and whorls of thin little branches rather like the spokes of an umbrella (and quite infertile) grow around nodes along the stems. This is the last of a family of plants that flourished during the Carboniferous period. It is a wild plant in temperate regions and will invade the garden, where it likes a dry and stony spot and, once in, it is hard to get out.

It does not produce flowers but increases from spores that are carried away on the wind.

MEDICINAL USE: Diuretic, astringent, stomachic, tonic, antiseptic.

Soak 1 ounce (30g) dried herb in 2½ cups (600mL) cold water for 2-3 hours then boil up and keep at a gentle rolling boil for at least 20 minutes. Strain well and take twice a day in wine-glassful doses for anemia and general low health, cystitis, dropsy, chest and lung complaints and any internal bleeding.

The leaves are efficacious if applied externally too. In addition to taking the decoction when a wound is bleeding heavily, apply a thick warm poultice of freshly picked and bruised horsetail. If you think your child may have picked up nits, wash the hair in a strong horsetail infusion and the eggs of the parasites will be killed off.

Horsetail has been said to dissolve tumors. The plant has a high silica content and is also rich in vitamins and minerals.

The variety known as "Dutch-rushes" was once used to scour brass, pewter and wooden vessels. If you have horsetail growing near you, it is worth giving it a try—the variety E. hyemale is the best one for this purpose but I have been unable to find out how to identify it. Any plant picked for use should be free of brown fungus spots and, once dried, only the stems that remain green should be retained for use.

COSMETIC USE

The silica in horsetail makes it a valuable nail nutrient. Oil the hands well, particularly the nails and cuticles, then soak the nails in warm horsetail "tea."

The cool tea also makes a good skin tonic.

IN THE GARDEN

Horsetail tea makes a good spray to use for mildew and fungus; sprayed lightly over young plants it will prevent them "damping off." Boil up a tablespoonful of dried leaves in 4 cups (1L) of water and hold at the boil for about 20 minutes. Let the liquid stand for 2 days covered, then strain well to prevent any bits clogging the nozzle of the sprayer.

HYSSOP

Botanical name: *Hyssopus officinalis*
Family: *Labiatae*
Part used: Whole plant

Hyssop, native to southeast Europe, will tolerate any temperate climate given a fair amount of sun. A pleasant bushy plant, it will grow to about 24 inches (60cm) high, with neat narrow leaves and bluish-mauve flowers (you can find white and pink varieties) and the whole plant gives off a scent somewhere between rosemary and camphor. Forget the camphor ball—hyssop scent is mintier and much more pleasant.

Propagation can be from seed if you are prepared to be patient or from cuttings and root division. The plant is a valuable asset to the herb garden and will make a good little hedge—but it is deciduous so you have to be prepared for late season leaf-drop—not that this matters when one sees how butterflies and bees hover over the plant while it is in flower.

CULINARY USE

The chopped leaves added to sausages and fat meats that are difficult to digest will render them less troublesome to a delicate stomach. If you like the flavor, try a few chopped pieces in soups, stews and even fruit pies. Go carefully—the flavor is quite pungent.

MEDICINAL USE: Stimulant, carminative, pectoral, febrifuge, anthelmintic.

"A decoction of Hyssope made with figges, honey, water and rue helpeth an olde cough" the old herbalist said and certainly the healing oil contained in hyssop has maintained a reputation down the centuries for ridding the body of mucus and easing all complaints of the respiratory tract. The oil is not only cleansing but antiseptic.

Do not use an infusion stronger than q ounce (20g) flowering tips to 4 cups (1L) boiling water or take more than 3 cupfuls a day. If you have a bad sprain, or if the pain of rheumatism plagues, or there is heavy bruising or a rough wound, bathe the affected parts and poultice with an infusion twice as strong. Soak pads of cotton wool in the infusion, squeeze gently to eliminate excess moisture, apply to the area, cover with oil-silk and bandage to retain the heat.

The antiseptic qualities of hyssop make it useful in widely dissimilar circumstances. It can be used as an eye-wash, a hair-wash when lice are present, a gargle for sore throat and quinsy, a gentle "wormer," a cleanser of a system plagued by jaundice, dropsy or an inactive spleen, and a soothing lotion for insect bites and stings.

COSMETIC USE

Commercially hyssop is valued in the perfume industry and the concentrated oil is often used in the manufacture of "eau-de-Cologne."

IN THE GARDEN

Hyssop tea makes a good spray to use for bacterial diseases. A border of hyssop around the cabbage patch will lure away the cabbage-moth. Grapevines thrive if hyssop is growing near them; radishes won't.

JUNIPER

Botanical name: *Juniperus communis*
Family: *Cupressus*
Parts used: Berries, leaves and wood

The gray-green leaf needles, cone-shaped flowers and typical scent make it obvious that juniper belongs to the pine family. It will grow straight and strong in a sheltered position and can reach 10 feet (3m) but will crouch low against a cold prevailing wind and make a stubby little bush of no more than 6½ feet (2m). It grows wild in many parts of the world and will be quite well-behaved in a garden in a temperate area.

There are male and female plants, recognizable by their different colored "flowers" that grow in the leaf axils. The male flowers are yellow, the female blue-green; the berries which follow them turn from green to a silvery blue-black. You can propagate from cuttings. The berries are easy to dry in the sun or a warm, airy spot.

CULINARY USE

When you drink gin, you are tasting the flavor of the juniper berry so you can judge whether you would like them in stuffings, pâte, marinades, sauerkraut, coleslaw, etc. Game dishes (venison, grouse, wild duck, hare, etc.) lose some of the "gamey" taste if a few berries are added—the taste is strong so you don't need many.

A leaf or so in the grill-pan under fish will give the food a light, pleasant flavor and any sausages, meat, etc. cooked on a barbecue on which juniper leaves or twigs are burning will also take on the juniper flavor.

MEDICINAL USE: Diuretic, stimulant, carminative, antiseptic, depurative.

Chewing juniper berries when traveling in tropical areas, or whenever and wherever there are epidemics of any sort, will help to ward off possible infection.

During flu epidemics, etc., at home, burn leaves and twigs in the house or throw some berries on the open fire—juniper is a great fumigant, so, if you have a heavy cold, draw the smoke into your lungs through the nostrils. An infusion of 1 ounce (30g) dried berries to 4 cups (1L) boiling water taken in cupful doses 3 times a day will relieve indigestion and wind, promote the flow of urine and the elimination of uric acid, disinfect the urinary tract and bile ducts, encourage sweating, and relieve cystitis. One precaution, though: while juniper is good for kidney and liver derangement, it should not be taken if there is any evidence of internal inflammation as it could be an irritant. Pregnant women should be very careful about any use of it. Externally a poultice made from the berries will relieve the pain of sciatica, lumbago, overstretched muscles and rheumatism. Juniper "tea" made from the twigs can be brewed and added to the bath water for the same reason.

LADIES' BEDSTRAW — Our Lady's Bedstraw, Cheese Rennet, Wild Rosemary

Botanical name: *Galium verum*
Family: *Rubiaceae*
Part used: Whole plant

The common names of this creeping perennial with its narrow shiny leaves that grow in a star-like whorl around the stem and panicles of golden-yellow flowers are as attractive as the plant itself. The scented flowers and neat leaves made it popular as a strewing herb in the Middle Ages and legend has it that Mary chose it to line her infant's crib. It was certainly used for a long time all over Europe as a stuffing for pillows and mattresses as it gives off a scent like lime-blossom or flower-honey.

At one time, particularly in the north of England, the stems and leaves were used instead of rennet to coagulate milk in the making of cheese and the yellow flowers gave the cheese its rich color.

Galium silvaticum is the white-flowered variety about which the early herbalists had little to say other than that poor women found it good for bathing sinews and joints to comfort and strengthen them after "travaile, cold or paines."

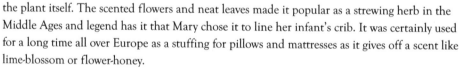

MEDICINAL USE: Diuretic, alterative, laxative.

An infusion made with 1 ounce (30g) leaves and 4 cups (1L) water and taken in wineglassful doses several times a day will promote urine, act as a laxative, help sufferers from "gravel" and settle the nerves. It is also good for the complexion.

The leaves, stems and flowers can be boiled up and the water used as a footbath after a day that has been heavy on the feet.

HOUSEHOLD USE

The creeping roots can be used to make a red dye.

LADY'S MANTLE — Lion's Foot, Dewcup

Botanical name: *Alchemilla vulgaris*
Family: *Rosaceae*
Part used: Whole plant

Lady's mantle likes the cold—it was once a sacred plant in Iceland and the early alchemists thought it had the ability to turn base metals into gold.

While it may not be as magical as all that, it has some remarkable properties.

It is a pretty plant although the greenish-yellow flowers are inconspicuous; the attraction lies in the leaf formation. The lobed leaves—the shape is rather like that of a lion's pad—are daintily toothed and softly hairy, and curved, so that moisture or dew is held in the shallow cup. They grow at the end of delicate slender stems. The plant is perennial with a black root and is essentially a plant of the northern hemisphere although the cultivated variety will grow in the shade in temperate areas in other parts of the world.

It is often thought of as "the woman's herb" as it was found to help conception and prevent miscarriage and the name "Lady's Mantle" came from the shape of the leaves—the gentle scallops being seen not only as a lion's foot but as the edges of the robe the Holy Mother probably wore.

CULINARY USE

The root is particularly astringent. The active constituent is tannin. Young leaves, although rather bitter, are not unpleasant in a salad.

MEDICINAL USE: Astringent, styptic, tonic.

An infusion of 1 ounce (30g) chopped whole plant or ⅔ ounce (20g) dried plant to 2½ cups (600mL) boiling water taken in teacupful doses several times a day will reduce excessive menstruation and diminish leucorrhoea—"whites."

Applied externally it is a good wound salve, cleansing, cooling and drying, and is therefore also good in desperate cases of adolescent acne.

LADY'S SLIPPER — Nerveroot, Yellow Lady's Slipper

Botanical name: *Cypripedium pubescens*
Family: *Orchidaceae*
Part used: Root

There are many different varieties of the Slipper Orchid—the neat, lovely and hardy member of the large orchid family—so make sure to ask for *C. pubescens* if you wish to grow it for medicinal purposes. The flower is yellow and the plant can be grown indoors or out—closely planted outdoors and in a smallish pot indoors for it prefers crowded conditions.

MEDICINAL USE: Antispasmodic, nervine, tonic.

The root, which tastes a bit like valerian, is used for nervous troubles such as hysteria, delirium, convulsions, insomnia, nervous exhaustion and irritability and is taken along with other herbal preparations for a "run-down" condition.

The root can be administered in powdered form or as a tincture and is more palatable when taken in water sweetened with a little honey.

LAVENDER

Botanical name: *Lavendula officinalis*
Family: *Labiatae*
Parts used: Flowers and leaves on the sprig or by themselves

Lavender, a native of the barren hills in the Mediterranean area, is now found in temperate climates all over the world and no wonder, for it is an elegant plant with a wonderful scent and many different uses. There are several different varieties in cultivation.

The lavenders make bushes that vary in size according to type and can have strong, twisted stems. The leaves are narrow and gray-green, a little downy, and when pressed between the fingers give off a scented oil; the flowers are spikes of tiny florets which lift from the plant on long stalks. The color is usually bluish-purple; the white variety is quite rare.

In the garden, lavenders like lime in the soil and plenty of sunshine; if it becomes necessary to give them water make sure any excess drains away.

Growing lavender from seed is a lengthy process but it can be done, propagation from stem cuttings is the most usual. To keep the bushes nicely shaped, trim them after the flowers have been cut. English lavender (*L. spica*) has the strongest colored flowers and makes a compact bush. There are dwarf varieties available, some with pinkish or pale-mauve flowers.

French and Spanish lavender both make quite hardy bushes but Italian lavender is more delicate and cannot take too much heat.

CULINARY USE

The scent of lavender is too sweet for most people for use with savory dishes although it is said to be quite pleasant in a hare stew. It makes a change from rosemary used with roast lamb or pork.

The flowers can be used to make lavender vinegar and lavender oil for use as salad dressings. A few blooms left in a sealed container of sugar for a few weeks (lumpy white sugar is best) make an unusual coffee sugar, and the crystallized flowers make a pretty cake decoration.

MEDICINAL USE: Sedative, carminative, vulnerary, antiseptic.

A tea made from the leaves and flowers has a gentle tranquilizing effect; bought lavender water can be very soothing when bathed on the temples in a case of headache of a nervous origin. Sniffing lavender oil will also help. Lavender oil can be made very simply; just leave a handful of bruised flowers in a clear glass bottle containing about 4 cups (1L) of olive oil in the sun for a few days and then strain. If the perfume is not strong enough, keep on repeating the process by adding more flowers to the strained oil until the desired strength is reached. Sucking a lump of sugar on which a few drops of oil have been poured is an old headache remedy.

The oil will also cleanse and heal wounds, burns, and stings for the essential element it contains is highly antiseptic, so much so that it can kill not only the streptococcus bacillus but also those of typhoid and diphtheria. Rubbed into the hair it will kill lice and their eggs; diluted and rubbed on the skin will give protection against mosquitoes, and into rheumatic joints some relief from pain. A weak lavender tea is said to make a good vaginal douche for leucorrhoea.

COSMETIC USE

If hair is thinning, try rubbing oil of lavender into the scalp.

HOUSEHOLD USE

The lavender bag or sachet has long been used to scent chest-drawers and their contents and to keep away moths, etc. The dried flowers are an essential part of any potpourri.

IN THE GARDEN

Lavender is very attractive to bees and is therefore of general benefit to the garden.

LILY—OF—THE—VALLEY — May Lily, Our Lady's Tears

Botanical name: *Convallaria majalis*
Family: *Liliaceae*
Part used: Whole plant, but mainly the root
Poisonous herb

All parts of this enchanting perennial plant are poisonous and it can be difficult to grow unless conditions are just right, but most gardeners welcome it for its sweetly-scented bell-shaped flowers and graceful elliptical leaves. There are pink and beige varieties but the pure white one, coming into flower as it does in spring, has a special appeal.

It grows wild in the woods of Europe and Asia where it finds the ideal conditions of shade, moisture and a soil rich in humus; these are the conditions it must have if it is to grow successfully in your garden—and it also needs some winter cold. If it takes well, it will spread and propagation can easily be made by digging up a clump and cutting the roots into pieces about 4 inch (10cm) square and replanting each one in a new position, preferably in autumn, but early spring will do too.

MEDICINAL USE: Cardiac, tonic, diuretic.

Since this is a poisonous plant, it goes without saying that the gardener should not attempt to make his own medicine from his plants. Country folk did, for long centuries, but we don't know how many mistakes were made. This is a valuable heart remedy with an action on the body like that of the digitalis in the foxglove but often preferred because it is gentler. It will strengthen and regulate heart action and balance the sympathetic nervous system, reduce cardiac dropsy, and, in stronger dosage, act as an emetic.

Since it has a generally quieting effect on the system it enables the brain to work more efficiently and thoughts to become clear instead of confused.

LIME — Linden
Botanical name: *Tilea*
Family: *Tiliaceae*
Parts used: Flowers, leaves and bark

While one hardly thinks of the lime tree as an "herb"; it is a splendid garden tree that provides many domestic remedies. There are both small- and large-leaved varieties and both have scented clusters of pale yellow flowers hanging from a brace. Although a native of Europe, it will grow in other temperate parts of the world.

CULINARY USE

The flowers have a light scent rather like that of the jonquil and are used both to make a refreshing "tea" for a hot day and a gentle sedative.

Beehives kept near lime trees produce a particularly delicious honey. The culinary and medicinal use of lime blossoms tends to merge.

MEDICINAL USE: Nervine, stimulant, tonic, diaphoretic, diuretic, antispasmodic, soothing.

The flowers dry easily in airy shade or can be bought, dried, at most health-food shops.

The infusion, made by pouring boiling water over the dried flowers, can be a little stronger than the "tea" and is taken to promote sweating in sufferers from influenza and bronchitis and will help to clear the bronchial tract. Tip any left over into the bath water.

If diarrhea is persistent or a nervous stomach is giving trouble or you can tell migraine is imminent, drink some lime tea.

The sapwood, reached by peeling away the dark brown shiny bark, is useful as a diuretic and aids both the liver and the kidneys, rheumatism, gout and sciatica. The leaves can be used to poultice sprains and swellings. When you find how useful the lime tree can be it is easy to understand why it once was planted by royal command to line roadways so that the blossoms could be collected for use in hospitals.

LICORICE

Botanical name: *Glycyrrhiza glabra*
Family: *Leguminosae*
Part used: Root

Licorice was known as a wild plant in southeast Europe and southwest Asia in ancient times and was actually grown as far north as Britain in the 16th century.

A pretty bushy perennial plant with finely divided leaves that fold as night falls and pale mauve or cream pea-type flowers, it needs a rich soil, hot summers and warm winters to be at its best. The root, which is the main reason the plant is grown commercially, becomes woody and not as pleasant in use under less favorable conditions. Licorice can be grown from seed but it is better to cut off a piece of root that carries a "bud" and plant that. If you are really into licorice, you could make a row of plants but set them at least 4 inches (10cm) below the soil and keep them well apart for the little bushes spread and the roots need space. You will have to be patient for the roots will not be ready for harvesting for 3 or even 4 years.

The "Spanish Juice" most children love is made commercially by extracting the juice from the root and solidifying it into sticks.

CULINARY USE

If you are terribly thirsty, try chewing some dried licorice root—this is hardly a culinary tip and you can make a refreshing drink by taking a little more trouble—just macerate some bruised peeled root (1¾ ounces/50g to 4 cups/1L of water) for at least 24 hours, then add some powdered ginger or aniseed or fennel, with honey or sugar to sweeten to taste. You can be as inventive as you like—slices of lemon can be floated in the liquid or lemon juice added if you like a sharper flavor.

A drink made with licorice, barley and dried couch grass root is rich in vitamins and minerals, pleasant in taste and said to be the most thirst-quenching drink you could offer a fretful patient or a parched athlete.

Soak licorice root overnight. Make barley water. Boil couch grass root for 10 minutes. Combine all liquids.

MEDICINAL USE: Demulcent, pectoral, expectorant, antispasmodic, laxative.

Licorice is remarkable in that it contains a natural hormone that acts like cortisone; when the blood sugar level falls too low, doses of licorice will restore it to normal, and yet diabetics, whose blood sugar level is often too high, have been found able to take licorice without ill effect. Its main usefulness, however, is in the relief of colds, coughs, sore throat, bronchial catarrh, on one hand and the soothing of the pain and cramp of stomach ulcers on the other. A decoction of 12 ounces (40g) bruised peeled root to 4 cups (1L) of water (keep on a low steady boil for at least 10 minutes) makes a sweetish pleasant drink, which can be sipped as needed. Remember that the bark is rather bitter, so if that bothers you be sure to peel the root first. Licorice is gently laxative. The old-fashioned lollies Licorice All-sorts and Pontefract cakes were even more pleasant to take than that great old stand-by, Syrup of Figs.

LOBELIA — Indian Tobacco, Pukeweed
Botanical name: *Lobelia inflata*
Family: *Campanulaceae*
Part used: Herb

The lobelia family, named for the Flemish botanist Matthias de Lobel, is a large one, remarkable for the fact that the stems of the plants produce latex, a milky juice. *L. inflata* is an annual plant that grows around 3 feet (1m) high with angular hairy leaves, slightly toothed pointed leaves and small-petalled pale-blue flowers. When the plant is burned it smells like tobacco. It is a native of the American eastern states.

MEDICINAL USE: Expectorant, emetic, anti-asthmatic, diaphoretic, stimulant.

The most important quality this plant possesses is its ability to enable the body to expel mucus. It is particularly useful for babies and children who have not learned how to "hawk" and get rid of the mucus, which could strangle breath.

For croup, asthma and whooping cough there is little better. Both the powdered herb and the liquid extract are obtainable commercially.

Lobelia can be used as a first line of defense in all liver and stomachic complaints as it is a de-obstruent and will clear the way for the use of more specific medicines. One ounce (30g) of the powdered herb made into an infusion with 2½ cups (600mL) boiling water should be taken in wineglassful doses for adults and quarter wineglassful doses for babies and children.

The powder, mixed with Slippery Elm powder, is good for any inflammation or swelling, particularly if ulceration is beginning to show.

Since there are many other members of the family and mistakes could be made, it is best to buy lobelia instead of using any garden plant.

LOVAGE — Smellage

Botanical name: *Levisticum officinale*
Family: *Umbelliferae*
Parts used: Leaves and root

Lovage is a tall, handsome slow-growing perennial with glossy green leaves rather like those of celery and umbels of pale yellow flowers, which the bees love. It does not germinate easily or grow well in cool weather but since one plant will furnish most family needs, it is well worth a try. Any climate similar to the Mediterranean type will suit it well enough given light shade, enough moisture and a friable soil.

The whole plant is aromatic. Leaves should be cut for drying before the flowers appear to get the best flavor and the seeds only gathered when they have become really brown. If you want to increase your stock, try root division.

CULINARY USE

Lovage has a strong, sharpish taste, a bit like yeast, and will warm and enrich vegetable soups and vegetarian dishes. A potato and onion soup is invigorated by the inclusion of lovage.

POTATO AND LOVAGE SOUP

Ingredients
2 onions, thinly sliced or chopped
½ cup lovage leaves snipped fine with scissors
1 pound (450g) small-diced potatoes
Plain flour

4½ cups (1 liter) water, or vegetable stock, or stock from chicken cube, etc., depending on personal taste. 1¼ cup (300mL) milk or mixed milk and cream
Chopped chives

Method

Sauté the onions in oil or bacon fat until soft, add lovage leaves. Stir in and continue to sauté. Add diced potatoes, cook and stir with a little flour for thickening but do not allow the flour to change color—3-4 minutes should be long enough. Add stock, season to taste, simmer until the diced potato breaks when prodded by a fork. Remove from heat, cool a little, then add milk or milk and cream. Purée in a blender. Serve the soup in individual bowls with a scattering of chopped chives as garnish.

A judicious amount of snipped leaf will enliven a salad or sauce.

The chopped stems and leaf-stalks can be used as a vegetable (a bit like celery) or candied (like angelica)—personally both exercises are only done to avoid waste as the flavor is not all that remarkable.

The seeds can be sprinkled over cakes and scones—they suit cheese scones particularly well.

MEDICINAL USE: Diureti, carminative.

Tea made from the young leaves is good for the relief of stomach wind, to stimulate the kidneys and ease cystitis. The ground seeds, which were once used like pepper, also make a warming drink—a little like Vegemite.

The old herbalist Gerard who claimed that the distilled water of lovage cleared the sight also said that liquid extract made from the root "driveth away ventosities or windinesse," and at the present time people in India chew the raw stems believing them to be a protection against cholera.

COSMETIC USE

The country name "smellage" was due to lovage's reputation as a deodorant. You can either add scrunched-up handfuls of the leaves and stems to the bath water or, as a rather less messy procedure, make a strong "tea" and pour that into the hot water just before you step in. The more elegant way is to make some little muslin bags and use as one would a teabag—in the bath. Each bag can be used at least twice. Drinking lovage tea or bathing in it, the result is the same—should desperation strike and there is no time to bathe or make tea, try tucking a few lovage leaves about the person.

The strong rather male scent of lovage makes it ideal for giving the distilled water to the men in your life plagued by spots or freckles.

MACE — see NUTMEG

MAIDENHAIR FERN — Venus Hair, Rock Fern

Botanical name: *Adiantum capillus-veneris*
Family: *Filices*
Parts used: Leaves and stems

The beautiful Maidenhair fern—of which there are many varieties—is well known as a houseplant, which can be very touchy to grow. A native of southern Europe, it requires moisture, shade and an acid soil that is well drained; it does not appreciate chemical fertilizers. It is less well known as a medicinal plant.

MEDICINAL USE: Pectoral, expectorant.

An infusion of 1 ounce (30g) chopped herb to 2½ cups (600mL) boiling water, taken in wineglassful doses, will relieve a troublesome cough, bronchial catarrh and asthma. A little honey will improve the flavor.

The tea can also be used as a rinse for dull and lifeless hair.

MALE FERN — Shield Fern

Botanical name: *Dryopteris filix-mas*
Family: *Polypodiaceae*
Parts used: Roots and leaves

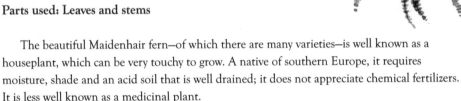

This fern, of which there are countless species, grows wild in the open woodland and shaded forests of Europe. The curled leaves, which grow in a rosette around the stem, open into fronds which can be as much as 3 feet (1m) tall, with the toothed leaves growing alternately on the stem and getting smaller toward the tip.

The shape of the plant is like that of a deep funnel. The root is strong and large—a rhizome with many fibrous roots—and it is for the root the plant has been mostly prized for so long.

MEDICINAL USE: Vermifuge

The powdered root, or the fluid extract made from it, will expel worms from the body—tapeworms included. The taste is unpleasant so if you can buy it in pill or capsule form so much the better. After taking the prescribed dose, an herbal purgative is recommended. Since the action is fairly strong, small children, pregnant women and invalids should not use this method. Sufferers from rheumatism, neuritis, gout and arthritis could try a hot compress of leaves on the painful parts, a "tea" in the bath water and an herbal pillow stuffed with the carefully dried leaves.

MARIGOLD — Pot Marigold

Botanical name: *Calendula officinalis*
Family: *Compositae*
Parts used: Petals and herb.

The annual marigold with its round gaudy flower-heads of yellow and orange is part of almost every summer garden in the northern hemisphere. It grows well in any temperate area and can adapt to almost any type of soil. The seeds can be sown in autumn if the plantlings can be kept sheltered and warm during the winter; otherwise sow in spring.

The bruised leaves give off a strong and acrid flavor, which some people love to sniff for its bracing cleanliness; the bright petals have a less aggressive taste and are mildly piquant. This plant has been well known and well used since Roman times. It is a good-tempered grower, gives lovely flowers for cutting, offers a range of colors which can be used in a garden "palette," and offers a range

of culinary, cosmetic and medicinal uses few other plants can. It blooms freely and generously—
the Romans called it "calendula" because it was in bloom every month of the year.

CULINARY USE

The dried petals give flavor to homemade cottage cheese, soups and stews, and look good
sprinkled over salads. Rice, cakes and puddings can be colored yellow much more cheaply by
using dried marigold petals instead of saffron.

MEDICINAL USE: Stimulant, diaphoretic.

An infusion of 1 ounce (30g) herb to 2½ cups (600mL) boiling water taken in wineglassful
doses will help ulcers and hepatitis; produce perspiration when a patient is fevered; applied
locally it will ease the pain of varicose veins, running ulcers, chilblains and any wound, burn or
scald. A tincture of calendula as an antiseptic for cuts, grazes, etc., is one of the best first-line
defenses any home could have.

You can buy calendula ointment but if you wish to make your own, simmer 4 ounces (120g)
of the orange petals freshly plucked from the flowers in ½ cup (150mL) water and 14 ounces
(400g) clean white lard. Keep simmering until the water has evaporated, being careful not to
let the mixture "catch." Strain well; pour into a jar and allow to cool before tightly corking or
otherwise stoppering.

Homoeopathic preparations of calendula are particularly valuable.

The crushed flowers will relieve the pain of bee or wasp sting; the crushed leaves applied to a
corn night and morning will gradually facilitate removal. A tincture made from the flowers can
be used instead of arnica for sprains and bruises.

COSMETIC USE

A rinse made from the flowers was once used to turn the hair golden; used on material it
produces a deep cream color.

MARJORAM — Joy of the Mountains

Botanical name: *Origanum marjorana*
Species: *O. onites, O. vulgare.*
Family: *Labiatae*
Parts used: Herb and leaves

The confusion between marjoram and oregano can be resolved by realizing that the cultivated marjoram comes from the wild oregano and that the first has a sweet flavor and the second a strong, tangy, peppery one. Both can be bought dried.

Sweet marjoram—knotted marjoram—makes a neat bushy plant about 10 inches (25cm) high with whitish-green leaves and small white flowers; there is also a creeping variety.

In the garden it requires a fairly dry chalky soil, full sun and no frost.

Since the seeds are very fine and the finnicky process of transplanting is required with close attention to watering and freedom from weeds, it may be simpler to buy a plant or two from a nursery and keep them either in the pots on a windowsill or transplant them into the herb garden. In cool climates the plant should be treated as an annual—in warmer ones it can be biennial or perennial. Pot marjoram—*O. onites*—makes a stronger clump, growing to about 20 inches (50cm) tall and is more spreading in habit. When the plant becomes too large it can be divided. Propagation can also be made from cuttings. The wild marjoram—*O. vulgare*—is a straggly plant with strong rhizomatous roots and is at home in dry, hot and stony ground in warmish climates. It is a favorite flavoring herb with the Italians, the Greeks and the Mexicans and is the most widely used of the species as a medicinal herb.

There are other members of the family, notably Dittany of Crete and Winter Marjoram. If plants can be obtained they are well worth a try in the garden.

CULINARY USE

The finely chopped leaves can be added to vegetables, salads, sauces, sandwiches, meat dishes, scones, omelets—once you like the flavor it can be a case of marjoram with everything. The dried herb has the stronger flavor.

A tasty herb vinegar can be made by filling a bottle with leaves and then pouring in wine or cider vinegar to the top. Cover and leave in the sun for at least 10 days; strain and rebottle; keep in a cool cupboard for use as required.

MEDICINAL USE: Tonic, emmenogoguic, stimulant.

Marjoram contains a volatile oil, which can be used internally and externally.

The wild variety gives the best oil for rubbing on bruises and sprains and it is very simply made. Bruise a fistful of the herb, cut up to manageable size with a touch of white or cider vinegar then add to a bottle of sunflower seed oil. Screw the bottle tightly, shake to distribute the oil and then leave in the sun or a constantly warm place for a few weeks, giving the bottle a shake every now and then. Strain and rebottle, keeping the seal tight to retain the fragrance.

Tea made from the leaves is both a tonic and a "soother" useful for digestive upsets, morning sickness, insomnia and vague aches and pains. Toothache can be eased by pressing bruised leaves around the tooth. A little pillow stuffed with the dried herb makes a fragrant aid to sleep and sachets of the dried herb make a sweet-smelling disinfectant for drawers left unused for too long.

COSMETIC USE

Strong marjoram "tea" makes a good hair tonic used as a conditioner after shampooing. Rub into the scalp and do not rinse off.

MARSHMALLOW — Mallards

Botanical name: *Althaea officinalis*
Family: *Malvaceae*
Parts used: Leaves and root

This northern hemisphere native grows wild in moist salty places and is cultivated in other parts of the world where the climate is suitable. It does not like a severe winter. A perennial plant, it can make more than 3 feet (1m) in height. The stem is thick and woody at the base, the gray-green leaves are toothed and softly hairy and 3-lobed. The flowers are a soft rose-pink and have 5 delicate petals; they grow in the leaf-axils.

A relation of the hollyhock, but far less spectacular, it makes a pleasant back-of-the-border plant, well known to country people for the medicinal quality of the thick yellow root, which, like the leaves, is richly mucilaginous.

MEDICINAL USE: Demulcent, emollient.

Marshmallow ointment can be bought at most health food shops and is useful for sore skin; the leaves can be made into a tea to bathe sore eyes. The root, which should be dug in the autumn for drying, can also be used fresh to make a hot poultice for any inflammation of the skin, muscles or joints. If the dried root is to be kept for any length of time care must be taken to keep it dry.

The old name for it, "Mortification root," was given because its cleansing and soothing action was so strong it prevented gangrene setting in.

Syrups sold for the relief of coughs and bronchitis often contain marshmallow. An infusion of 1 ounce (30g) leaves to 2½ cups (600mL) boiling water, taken frequently in wineglassful doses, will help cystitis even when there is blood in the urine. It will also soothe colitis.

MEADOWSWEET — Queen of the Meadow, Lady of the Meadow, Bridewort, Dolloff
Botanical name: *Spireae ulmaria*
Family: *Rosaceae*
Part used: Whole plant

Meadowsweet is one of the loveliest of European wild plants. In summer, ditches, hedgerows, damp meadows and the banks of rivers and streams are graced by this tall plant with its pale froth of fragrant blossom and dark green serrated leaves which are silvery and downy on the underside. There is something magical about its scent.

Queen Elizabeth I "did more desire it than any other sweet herbe to strew her Chambers withal..." so the old herbalists tell us. The flowers have a rich, honeyed scent; the leaves are less heady; when dried they have the clean fragrance of new-mown hay. A few leaves of meadowsweet as a bookmark hold the scent of summer for months. Dropwort (*Filipendula hexapetula*) is another member of the family but only grows to about 8 inches (45cm) in height to contrast to the 6½ feet (2m) of its relation and it likes a drier soil. Either plant makes a lovely addition to the garden in a temperate climate and can be propagated by root division.

CULINARY USE

Since the plant is rich in Vitamin C, homemade herb beers benefit by the addition of a few flowers and leaves.

MEDICINAL USE: Aromatic, astringent, diuretic.

A tea made from the flowers and leaves is useful for a feverish cold or a digestive upset. It brings on perspiration. The astringent quality will also help troublesome diarrhea. The flower contains salicylic acid, an ingredient of aspirin, so it is easy to see why the tea can be used to ease the nerves or the pain of rheumatism and arthritis, etc. A decoction made by boiling the root is a good wound salve.

COSMETIC USE

The flowers, soaked in water in the sun and then strained and used as a face-wash, will soften and clear the complexion.

MELILOT — King's Clover, Hart's Clover

Botanical name: *Melilotus officinalis*
Family: *Leguminoseae*
Parts used: Flowers and leaves

This biennial grows wild in many temperate parts of the world and has been prized down the generations both as a fodder crop and for its

medicinal value. The plant grows about a 3 feet (1m) in height with branched stems of dark leaves that grow in threes and have spikes of small yellow pea-type flowers growing from the axils. The flowers and leaves give off a sweet scent that makes them very attractive to bees.

CULINARY USE

The country name, Hart's clover, reflects the use made of the plant in the cooking of rabbit. It is also used to flavor herb beers, stuffings and marinades.

MEDICINAL USE: Antispasmodic, emollient, carminative, sedative, antiseptic, diuretic.

A tea made from the dried flowering tips will relieve flatulence, insomnia, menstrual pain and retention of urine and can also be used to bathe sore eyes.

A strong infusion is good for swellings and sores. But probably its best-known use is as a tonic for the veins, helping to strengthen the venous walls. Varicose-vein sufferers will benefit by a regular intake of melilot tea.

HOUSEHOLD USE

Dried melilot leaves will scent the wardrobe and keep away moths.

MINT

Botanical name: *Mentha*
Family: *Labiatae*
Part used: Leaves

There must be around 40 different species of mint so it is necessary to confine this list to the ones best known. It is hardly needful to describe this familiar friend, which has been known and used since before the time of Christ.

Mint is a creeping plant with square stems, aromatic leaves and whorls of purplish-white flowers; all varieties have the same properties and the same needs, although in varying degree. Mints will not grow well in a dry soil; the common garden mint can take more sun than its relations and will grow leggy in the shade. When growing any of the mints a good rule of thumb is to make sure the soil is fairly rich and well limed, that sun and shade are well balanced and a water supply is handy. If you grow more than one species, keep them separate or they will hybridize and individual flavor will be lost.

All mints are intrusive; the easy way out is to grow them in pots although there is little nicer than a good healthy bed of mint. Propagation is easy—just pull up a good section of well-rooted stem, cut off and replant or you could take a spade and sever a thick clump into several pieces and replant those. Some species have an unfortunate tendency to develop rust; if you see the tell-tale brown marks on the leaves, get rid of the plant.

CULINARY USE

Spearmint (M. *spicata*) is the best culinary mint; the oval leaves are deep-green and hairless.

A few mint leaves added to the water in which vegetables are cooking—new potatoes and green peas in particular—give a clean, fresh flavor. Dried mint leaves in a little bag can also be used.

Mint sauce is good with cabbage and cauliflower as well as with lamb dinners, and mint jelly makes a nice change from the ubiquitous sauce.

Mint sauce is quickly made by boiling up finely chopped mint leaves with some white sugar and briefly holding at the boil before adding white vinegar to taste—there should, of course, be twice as much vinegar as water in the completed sauce. A quick mint jelly is made by pouring boiled well-sweetened vinegar over chopped mint leaves and some green jelly crystals or cubes. It can be made more exotic by a healthy dash of sweet sherry. Mix with redcurrant jelly for serving with lamb.

A mint jelly for keeping and storing is made using apples.

MINT JELLY

Ingredients

2 ounces (50g) tart apples

2 cups finely chopped mint

22 cups (600mL) water

Juice of 1 lemon and a little very finely grated rind

Granulated sugar

Method

Simmer the cut-up apples, cores and skins, in the water until reduced to pulp. Hang to strain in a muslin bag—don't squeeze the bag at any time. Add 1 pound (450g) sugar per 22 cups

(600mL) juice and boil carefully until thickened nicely. Allow to cool then add the chopped mint and lemon. The jelly will look more attractive though not taste any better if a few drops of green food coloring are added. Pour into warm, sterilized jars, seal and store.

Mint tea is a healthy cooling drink and a few mint leaves enliven almost any fruit drink. The famous alcoholic drink, the julep, owes its appeal less to the bourbon it contains than the sugar, mint leaves and ice.

Yogurt and chopped mint leaves make a good salad dressing.

Chopped mint can be added to soft cheese, chutneys and relishes; you can be as inventive as you like with mint, it is even good with mashed dates and a touch of lemon juice as a sandwich filling.

Bruised mint leaves can be added to a bottle of vinegar and then left to stand for a fortnight to make a vinegar just as pleasant as the more famous tarragon vinegar.

Lemon marmalade tastes even better with the addition of some finely-chopped mint leaves.

Apple mint (M. suaveolens) has small, downy leaves that can be variegated, and tiny pink flowers. It gives off an apple fragrance and makes a lovely ground cover. Since the leaves are so woolly, it is less popular as a culinary herb.

Another suaveolens variety is the pineapple mint, which, of course, smells like pineapple.

Orange bergamot mint (M. p. citrata) has red-tinged stems and smooth dark-green, red-edged leaves and purple flowers. It has a strong citrus flavor. The leaves can be chopped and added to salads.

MEDICINAL USE: Digestive.

Peppermint (M. *piperita*) comes in two varieties, black and white; the black has a purplish stem and purplish leaves, the white has a green stem and leaves, both are valuable for their oil, which contains menthol.

Tea made from the leaves is good for indigestion and vomiting, chewing a few leaves can relieve toothache; sweeten the breath. Quickly applied, bruised, to a bee or wasp sting they will take away the pain.

COSMETIC USE

Eau-de-Cologne mint gives off the recognizable odor of eau-de-Cologne so if a tea made from the leaves is added to the bath or washing water one has an inexpensive, fragrant toiletry.

A few leaves of this mint give a potpourri a lasting fragrance.

HOUSEHOLD USE
Mice do not like the scent of mint.

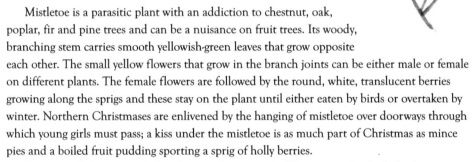

MISTLETOE
Botanical name: *Viscum album*
Family: *Loranthaceae*
Part used: Leaves

Mistletoe is a parasitic plant with an addiction to chestnut, oak, poplar, fir and pine trees and can be a nuisance on fruit trees. Its woody, branching stem carries smooth yellowish-green leaves that grow opposite each other. The small yellow flowers that grow in the branch joints can be either male or female on different plants. The female flowers are followed by the round, white, translucent berries growing along the sprigs and these stay on the plant until either eaten by birds or overtaken by winter. Northern Christmases are enlivened by the hanging of mistletoe over doorways through which young girls must pass; a kiss under the mistletoe is as much part of Christmas as mince pies and a boiled fruit pudding sporting a sprig of holly berries.

Long regarded as a sacred plant because it can sustain life on trees that look dead, many superstitions have grown up around it. The Druids cut it with a golden sickle in a yearly ceremony and the sprigs were worn as a talisman against evil spirits and hung in doorways to prevent their entrance.

MEDICINAL USE: Nervine, diuretic, antispasmodic.

The berries are widely regarded as poisonous but the leaves make excellent medicine in cases of epilepsy, high blood pressure and arteriosclerosis. Heat destroys their active properties so it is best to soak a good handful of the leaves in cold water for 12 hours and take in large wineglassful doses.

The dried powdered leaves can be used mixed with honey to ease a dry, tickling cough and are said to be good for whooping cough because of their antispasmodic property. Anyone nervous of using mistletoe as a home remedy should be able to find proprietary medicines that contain it.

MOTHERWORT — Lion's Ear, Lion's Tail, Herb of Life

Botanical name: *Leonurus cardiaca*
Family: *Labiatae*
Part used: Herb

This member of the nettle family grows wild in the northern hemisphere. The stems are square, the dark-green leaves are serrated with prominent veins underneath and are lightly hairy. The pink flowers grow in whorls in the leaf-axils at the top of the stems.

MEDICINAL USE: Tonic, nervine, antispasmodic, emmenogoguic.

This is one of the best-known female tonics. It acts on the generative organs as well as the heart and is so gentle a tonic it can be tolerated when stronger ones are not. It is excellent for the irritability of overstrain, the "shakes" and suppression of the menses due to general weakness. It can be bought in both powdered form and as a liquid extract.

MUGWORT — St John's Plant

Botanical name: *Artemesia vulgaris*
Species: *A. Lactiflora, A. ludoviciana*
Parts used: Roots and leaves

The Common mugwort (*A. vulgaris*) flourishes in the wild in rubble and waste places in many parts of the world but nevertheless can make a lovely garden plant attractive to bees.

A relative of wormwood and tarragon, mugwort is cultivated in the Middle East as an aromatic bitters supplier. All varieties of the plants grow tall and have deeply-cut ornamental leaves, gray in the case of A. *ludoviciana*, and dark-green otherwise. A. *vulgaris* has grooved, reddish stems with yellow flowers in panicles at the end of spikes; A. *lactifolia* has white panicles of sweetly-scented flowers; both varieties are attractive in the border and make good vase flowers. A. *ludoviciana* has unremarkable flowers but the soft, pale leaves that feel like felt are very pleasant seen against bright-colored flowers of another species.

You can propagate all plants from cuttings or root division.

CULINARY USE

Though not in the same class as tarragon the leaves can be used to tenderize meat and give an added piquance to the flavor. Mugwort is used commercially to flavor absinth and vermouth.

MEDICINAL USE: Emmenogoguic, diuretic, diaphoretic, vermifuge.

Mugwort is best known for its ability to promote the menstrual flow; it can be used in an infusion of no more than 1 ounce (30g) leaves to 22 cups (600mL) boiling water in cupful doses or used with Pennyroyal and Southernwood, two other herbs which have similar qualities.

This tea is also said to ease the pain of sciatica, although a more palatable and swifter remedy is the powdered leaves taken in wine.

The Greeks and Romans knew it as a sovereign remedy for the troubles of the menopause and a weak infusion taken for a few days each month can prove very helpful. Sustained use is not recommended because of the sedative effect. It is however a good simple tonic when appetite fails or the digestion is upset. The dried root is considered a safer and less drastic remedy than wormwood for the expulsion of worms but, if you buy any, use it at once as it quickly grows moldy.

After a long day, tired feet will appreciate a soaking in hot water with a strong infusion of mugwort leaves.

MULLEIN — Blanket Herb, Lady's Foxglove, Hag's Taper, Beggar's Blanket, Cow's Lungwort, Bullock's Lungwort, Our Lady's Flannel

Botanical name: *Verbascum thapsus*
Family: *Scrophulariaceae*
Parts used: Flowers and leaves

From the number of country names—of which the ones given are only a few—it can be seen that mullein is a plant no one has been able to ignore, and very splendid it is too. A biennial, it grows wild in the temperate zones of the world, flourishing in waste places, tolerant of both hot sun and lack of rain, its huge spike of yellow flowers rising on a flowering stem often more than 6½ feet (2m) tall, from a thick rosette of lanceate leaves at ground-level. Both stems and leaves are thickly covered with whitish-yellow down. Below the ground the root goes deep into the soil. The plant is so handsome it is easy to see why it is cultivated in many parts of the world. Legend has it that mullein made Ulysses proof against the blandishment of Circe; how he made use of the plant is not clear—but it is still believed in some quarters that it is a narcotic anodyne, a breaker of spells.

Mullein can be grown from seed but the seedlings must be transplanted well apart to give needed space and the ground should be dry rather than moist. The thick hairs the plant carries show it has plenty of mucilage and so does not lose its moisture through evaporation. Do not expect flowers until the second year.

MEDICINAL USE: Demulcent, expectorant, astringent, gently sedative.

An infusion of 1 ounce (30g) flowers and leaves to 2½ cups (600mL) boiling water taken in cupful doses will ease and loosen a stubborn cough, soothe inflammation when used as a gargle, reduce diarrhea and hay fever and make a good nightcap for insomniacs. It is important, however, to strain the tea very well because any hairs left in it could cause irritation. The same stricture applies if the leaves are used as a poultice for "sinews stiff and cold with cramp" or a skin inflammation; it is best not to apply the poultice directly to the skin but to use two layers of tightly-woven cloth as protection. A strong decoction, well strained, is probably wiser.

COSMETIC USE

The yellow flowers infused in boiling water and left until cool make a good rinse for fair hair which is beginning to lose its bright color.

OTHER USE

In the old days farmers used to give their cows tea made from the leaves when they developed chest trouble—hence the name "Cow's lungwort" or "Bullock's lungwort."

MUSTARD

Botanical name: *Brassica nigra*
Species: *B. alba*
Part used: Seeds

The mustards are annual plants that can grow to 62 feet (2m) in height; they have spiky leaves and bright yellow flowers with the calyx and corolla growing in the cruciform pattern typical of the species. The black variety makes a larger plant than the white one.

Charlock—wild mustard—Sinapis arvensis—is not considered here.

Hedge mustard—Sisymbrium officinale—a much smaller plant and though once recognized as an herbal remedy is not considered either.

The plants are grown for their seeds, which, in the case of the black mustard, are oval to round, and reddish-brown; white mustard seeds are slightly larger, globular and yellowish. They are all quite small. Sow the seeds in spring in sandy soil, in full sun; in late summer, when the seedpods have turned brown but have not split open, pick them and spread out in a warm, airy spot out of doors. When the pods are completely dry, shell the seeds. Do not allow the plants to self-seed or you will be overrun by them.

CULINARY USE

The seed of the black mustard has a fierier taste than that of the white variety. The bought dried English mustard is usually a combination of the two with the addition of turmeric to give added color—the flavor can be strong and hot, or mild. The Continental mustards—French, Dijon, German—follow individual recipes and often incorporate wine, sugar and herbs. American mustard is sweeter.

Some commercial mustards are smooth; others are nutty since the seeds are only coarsely ground; the variety is wide. It is very easy to make mustards to your own taste, either plain or with the addition of herbs, etc. The seeds, used whole, can be added to meat casseroles, pickles and salads—go gently, although when you bite into a seed it is not as eye-watering as you might think.

Dry mustard can be used in cooking but the bought mustards tend to separate and make the dish look rather messy. When making mustard for keeping always use sterilized jars as you would for jam-making—and keep the pots in the refrigerator.

SMOOTH MUSTARD

Ingredients

2 tablespoons dry mustard powder

Salt

2 dessert spoons sugar

2 eggs

Small teacupful any wine or herb vinegar

Method

Mix the mustard, salt and sugar; beat eggs, add the vinegar. Blend the two mixtures carefully and cook over gentle heat, stirring all the time until thick and smooth. Pot when cool.

NUTTY MUSTARD

Ingredients

1 cup mustard seeds

1 dessertspoonful black peppercorns
(you may need less according to taste)

2 teaspoonfuls dried herbs

1 cup salad oil

1 cup white vinegar

1 cup dry white wine

salt

Method

Grind salt and peppercorns together, add wine and stir well. Mix oil, vinegar and seeds together then combine the two mixtures stirring vigorously. Add herbs and stir again. Pot in sterilized jars and store for a week before use.

The easiest way to make an herb mustard is to use a bought jar of plain mustard and beat a little sugar, some brandy or wine, a little cream and your choice of finely chopped herbs into it. Keep in the refrigerator.

Slightly more time-consuming is to pound together in a mortar and pestle equal quantities black and white mustard seeds with some salt and pepper and a good sprinkling dried orange or lemon peel (a little of each is good). When as smooth as you can make it add a little honey and some cider vinegar and stir well. You can add a little turmeric for color.

MEDICINAL USE: Stimulant, diuretic, emetic, irritant.

There is nothing better, when chilled, than a hot bath containing mustard powder.

The volatile oil contained in the seeds is a powerful irritant and brings the blood to the surface of the skin and aids circulation. A poultice of mustard mixed with bran was a favorite old-fashioned remedy for a rusty chest or rheumaticky joints and muscles.

If, for some reason, it is necessary to induce vomiting, a cup of warm water into which dried mustard powder has been carefully stirred should be drunk as quickly as possible. The whole seeds, washed down with a little water, act as a laxative.

MYRTLE

Botanical name: *Myrtus communis*
Family: *Myrtaceae*
Parts used: Leaves, flowers and berries

This tall evergreen shrub grows well in temperate climates and has glossy dark green aromatic leaves and creamy-white, many-stamened scented flowers which are followed by berries that look rather like those of the black currant. Given sun and protection from frost it makes a handsome addition to the garden and can easily be propagated from cuttings or by layering.

CULINARY USE

The dried leaves and berries can be used in stuffings for hare or venison and a fresh branch on the barbecue coals will flavor the sausages or meat cooked above them.

MEDICINAL USE: Pulmonary.

A tea made from the powdered leaves is useful in chest complaints and can check night sweats.

HOUSEHOLD USE

The dried flowers can be added to a potpourri mixture.

NASTURTIUM – Indian Cress, Flower of Love

Botanical name: *Tropaeolium majus*
Family: *Tropaeolaceae*
Parts used: Leaves, flowers and seeds

A native of Peru, the nasturtium is now at home in gardens all over the world and is one of the easiest of all flowers to grow from seed. It is a highly ornamental plant, tolerant of poor soil, but it does like the sun. If your ground is too rich you will get leaves rather than flowers and a rather inelegant sprawl of juicy stems. The leaves are a clean green, flat, and round or kidney-shaped; the helmet-shaped flowers can range in color from sharp yellow, through orange to a rich scarlet with some delightful tones between. It is a splendid plant for giving color to a garden right through a long flowering season.

CULINARY USE

The leaves, which are rich in Vitamin C, have a pleasantly sharp taste and will liven a plain salad—so will the flowers and seeds. A little cream cheese tucked into a nasturtium flower makes a tasty snack.

The seeds can be pickled and used instead of caper sauce—good with cold lamb or boiled meat. They are however gently purgative and diuretic so be moderate. The shredded leaves give flavor to sandwich fillings and will take away the tired taste of mushrooms that have been kept too long before cooking. If the doctor has forbidden you to use salt and you miss it, try nasturtium leaves as a "lift" to appetite.

Nasturtium vinegar, which is very good with fish, is made by filling a large jar with the flowers and adding vinegar to cover with some salt and pepper—cayenne makes it more interesting. Cover and leave for a day or two when you will find the flowers will have sunk leaving room for more vinegar. Top up, seal and leave in a cool place for a fortnight. Strain and bottle. Store in the refrigerator.

The seeds can be pickled and used as one would capers.

PICKLED NASTURTIUM SEEDS

Ingredients

8 ounces (225g) nasturtium seeds 2 cloves

1 teaspoonful ground nutmeg   2 cups (0.5L) cider vinegar

Method

Boil cloves and nutmeg in the vinegar and hold briefly at boiling point before pouring, strained, over the seeds. A little salt is good with this but, for a salt-free diet, it can be omitted. Keep in a tightly covered jar for 3 weeks to a month before using to allow the flavor to mature.

MEDICINAL USE: Antibiotic, diuretic, purgative tonic.

The plant contains large amounts of sulfur and is a natural antibiotic that does not destroy the intestinal flora. If you are allergic to penicillin or are against it for any reason and are troubled with boils, abscesses, hangnails, or any skin infection, use the crushed fruits as a hot poultice and drink a tea made from the leaves—a small handful, chopped, to a cup of boiling water made fresh 3 times a day. This tea makes a good face-wash for acne-sufferers and is also good for bronchitis and emphysema.

If other laxatives cause griping, try the dried, crushed seeds either washed down or mixed with jam or honey.

COSMETIC USE

For dull hair which comes out on the comb, use a lotion made by macerating equal quantities freshly picked nasturtium flowers and leaves, fresh nettle leaves and fresh box leaves—

all well chopped—in some alcohol from the chemist for a fortnight. Don't worry if you can't find the box leaves, just use the first two. Strain well—add a touch of perfume if you like—and rub into the scalp frequently.

IN THE GARDEN

Nasturtiums secrete a mustardy oil which insects find attractive so plant them near your cabbage, cauliflower, broccoli, brussels sprouts, kohlrabi, turnips and cucumber and your crop will be spared much depredation.

Nasturtiums growing near radishes will improve their flavor.

NETTLE

Botanical name: *Urtica dioica*
Species: *U. urens, U. pilulifera*
Parts used: Flowers, leaves, seeds and roots

The nettle has been known all over the temperate regions of the world since time immemorial—how many million bare legs must have been stung by brushing against those hairy leaves so rich in formic acid! All varieties of the plant sting—*U. pilulifera*, which the Romans introduced into England, is the most vicious. *U. dioica* is a tall perennial; *U. urens* a smaller annual. *U. dioica* is the best known. The tall square stems of this variety can grow 3 feet (1m) high and, like the dark-green serrated leaves, are covered with fine hair. There are male and female plants. The male flowers are green, erect catkins, the female are longer and droop downwards. *U. urens* has male and female flowers on the same plant.

The wind scatters the seed and the tough roots creep along underground, throwing up stems as they go.

Though nettles are hardly decorative and the tidy gardener is usually quick to root out an invader, they are among the most valuable plants to man, offering food and medicine and help in the garden most generously.

CULINARY USE

It is best to wear gloves while collecting nettles for cooking. Pick only the youngest leaves and the tips—the older leaves can be used for other purposes.

Before using, soak the leaves, etc., in water for a minute or two to draw the sting out, then shake lightly and cook as spinach and serve with plenty of seasoning and butter. A few seconds taken in chopping them really well is worthwhile.

Soup made by sautéing chopped onion and young chopped nettle leaves and tips before boiling until tender should be thickened before serving. Stock, milk if you prefer it, and flour or arrowroot, made into a paste, should be carefully mixed with a little of the hot water before stirring in and cooking until nicely thick. Add a good dob of butter and serve.

This is good healthy food. Nettles contain chlorophyll, protein, iron, silica, sulfur, potassium, sodium and some Vitamin A, B and C.

NETTLE BEER

Country people have many different recipes. They boiled up their nettle tops, etc., in iron saucepans, thereby adding more iron to the drink. Today it is probably necessary to use a stainless steel or enamel saucepan—aluminum ones should not be used.

You will need at least 2 pounds (1kg) of fresh nettle tips, etc., to 1 gallon (4L) water, a good cup of lemon juice and 1 pound (450g) raw sugar. I like an addition of ground ginger, 2 teaspoonfuls is on the generous side. Boil all together for 20 minutes. Strain into a pan or dish with a pouring lip and allow to cool to a gentle heat. Mix 2 teaspoonfuls fresh yeast with a little of the liquid and stir in. Alternatively spread the yeast on a piece of toasted bread and gently lower it to float on top of the liquid. Cover and keep warm and out of draughts for 3-4 days. Then bottle, hammering down the cork firmly and leave in a dark cupboard for 10 days. Uncork with care.

MEDICINAL USE: Astringent, diuretic, tonic, haemostatic, vermifuge, emmenogoguic-

depurative, anti-anaemic, anti-diabetic, stimulant, irritant.

Nettles are so useful it is difficult to know where to start.

A tea made from the young leaves is an excellent tonic and will clear impurities from the blood, stimulate the digestion, rid the body of excess water, help to reduce blood sugar, ease rheumatism, reduce kidney stones, increase the menstrual flow, and if the young leaves themselves (boiled) are pressed on a bleeding wound they will stem the flow of blood and ease bruises. A tea made from the root is good for any internal bleeding. If you have a juicer, try the fresh juice of the leaves as well. Nettle juice on cotton wool makes a nasal plug which will stop a nosebleed very quickly. The fresh leaves, rubbed on painful rheumatic spots, will sting like mad but ultimately bring relief. The Romans, miserable and cramped by the damp chill of the country they had come to dominate, restored circulation by whipping their legs with the heavily-leaved stems. Just rubbing will suffice. If all other rheumatic remedies have given scant relief, it is worth trying this simple exercise—severe it may be but so many people in the past have found it their best bet that it is surely worth enduring a little discomfort each day to find real improvement in a wearisome condition.

The seeds are claimed to help bed wetters. The easy way to take them is in a spoonful of jam or honey before cleaning the teeth and going to bed.

The homoeopathic remedy "urtica," which is made from nettles, is one of the sovereign kitchen first aids. Applied to a burn or scald just received, it has an almost miraculous ability to take away pain and enable the skin to heal without scarring.

COSMETIC USE

Nettle tea made by boiling up the roots, and nettle juice can be used when hair is falling out or dandruff persists. Strain the tea and rub into the scalp each morning. I am told the nettle juice should be combed through the hair but whether it is left to dry or is rinsed off I have been unable to discover. It is said to restore the hair to its natural color—presumably in the case of brunettes.

IN THE GARDEN

Nettle tea made from the leaves can be used as a spray against aphids and as a plant tonic. Allow a few nettles to grow among your tomato plants to help them to escape mold. If you have a bed of nettles, don't pull them out and burn them, drop them into a pot left to catch rainwater and leave for 3 weeks; the ensuing brew will be rich in nourishment plants need. Failing this just chop them up and dig them into the soil or add them to the compost heap. Never waste a nettle.

OTHER USES

Add chopped nettles to chicken, pig and horse food. Add nettle seeds to poultry mash. Cheap, easy and highly nutritious—the proof will soon be seen.

NUTMEG

Botanical name: *Myristica fragrans*
Family: *Myristicaceae*
Part used: Seeds

Nutmeg and mace are often confused. Nutmeg is the dried kernel of the fruit of the tree; mace is the covering that surrounds it. The flavors are much the same, but mace is less sweet.

The tree, a native of the Molucca Islands, is also found in other parts of Indonesia and the West Indies. Tall, evergreen, with a smooth pale bark, dark-green pointed leaves and small yellow flowers, which are followed by a fleshy fruit that contains the seed in its surrounding "aril"—mace—the tree is long-lived and gives more than one crop of seeds a year. The nutmeg and the mace are dried separately and since insects like nutmeg, it is sometimes treated with lime for protection.

Always buy nutmegs whole; they lose flavor when cut. Since they vary in quality, test the ones on offer by cutting through; the color should be a variegated brown and white and there should be a film of oil on the knife. Mace, which is bought in "blades," should exude oil when pierced.

CULINARY USE

Since mace is less sweet than nutmeg, it is best used with savory dishes; nutmeg is a good cake and pudding spice, used either alone or mixed with other sweet spices. Ground mace powder or freshly grated nutmeg can be sprinkled over stewed fruit, mashed potatoes, carrots, etc. If people like the flavor—and the Dutch do—it can be a case of nutmeg with everything. On a cold day a hot chocolate drink liberally spiced with powdered nutmeg can be a great comforter.

MEDICINAL USE: Carminative, stomachic.

Used in small quantities, powdered nutmeg will ease stomach wind, stop vomiting, and gently soothe the nervous system; taken in large amounts, it can have an effect similar to that of mescaline or the amphetamines. Take the powder of two nutmegs at one time and you could be dead. As a nightcap brandy, nutmeg will induce peaceful sleep and calm the digestion. Grate a whole nutmeg into 2½ cups (600mL) brandy and leave to steep for at least a fortnight. A glass of hot milk with a strained tablespoonful of the mixture tastes good and is gently sedative.

OREGANO — see MARJORAM

ORRIS — White Flower de Luce

Botanical name: *Iris florentina*
Family: *Itidaceae*
Part used: Root

This white-flowered member of the Iris family is a native of the eastern Mediterranean area and can be grown in any similar climatic area. The leaves are the typical Iris blade-shape and can grow up to 3 feet (1m) in height. Propagation is by division of the thick rhizomatic root. The flowers have a light scent; the root, which gives the plant its importance, has little scent when fresh but develops a clean violet fragrance as it dries; the oil is used commercially in the production of violet scents.

HOUSEHOLD USE

Orris powder is the main fixative used in the making of potpourri, scented sachets of dried flowers and herbs and pomanders. It can be bought at most chemist shops. If you dry your own root, make certain it is dry before you attempt to grind it and keep any powder not used at once in a well-stoppered jar.

See index for the making of potpourri, etc.

PANSY — Heartsease
Botanical name: *Viola tricolor*
Family: *Vilaceae*
Part used: Whole plant

That the wild pansy won its place in the medicinal herbal is shown by the country name it was given—Heartsease.

It grows wild in the temperate parts of the world—an annual plant, it has cup-shaped serrated leaves and is easily recognizable by the flowers, which are yellow, white or lavender-striped with the two upper petals of the flowers erect and the others curving downward. Grown in the garden, it is pretty but inconspicuous.

MEDICINAL USE: Diuretic, expectorant, depurative, nervine.

A tea made from the dried leaves will clear the skin by cleansing the blood and ridding the system of excessive water; it will release phlegm and cleanse the urinary tract. A quick wound salve is made by pressing the dried leaves on the damaged flesh.

A tea made from the whole plant is good for nervous fears and exhausted nerves. Use leaves, stems and flowers.

PARSLEY

Botanical name: *Petroselinium crispum*
Family: *Umbelliferae*
Parts used: Leaves, stems and roots

Parsley is one of the great garden herbs and, however much is grown, there never seems to be enough. It has obviously always been a tricky herb to establish because legend says the seed must go to the Devil and back seven times before the plant will grow. A biennial with dark green leaves, either plain or curly, it takes a long time to germinate and some impatient gardeners give up on it too soon.

If the seed is soaked in warm water before sowing, it will speed germination by softening its tough coating.

A native of the Mediterranean area, parsley is now grown all over the temperate parts of the world—the plain-leaved variety will survive a vicious winter much better than the curly one. Although mainly used as a food garnish, the plant is rich in vitamins and minerals, proteins, iron and calcium and its inclusion in the diet can do nothing but good. It is not widely realized that apart from the Vitamins A, B and C contained in the leaves and stems, the roots are an even richer source of Vitamin C than oranges. The Hamburg variety has the largest roots—they can even be used as a vegetable. Parsley needs a rich soil containing plenty of humus, no more than 50 percent sun and plenty of water. The leaves should always be picked regularly, from the outside of the plant, and any flowering stem should be nicked off on sight. Some people treat it as an annual because the flowers appear in its second year of growth and they don't want the trouble, and naturally the plant is beginning to put its strength toward the formation of seeds.

CULINARY USE

As a garnish the leaves can be used whole, chopped or even fried. When adding parsley to soups, stews, casseroles, sauces and stuffings, always include the chopped stems—they are full of flavor and nutriment.

Parsley sauce is almost mandatory for fish dishes. A highly nutritious soup can be made using chicken stock.

PARSLEY SOUP

Ingredients

chicken stock	cream
chopped parsley	salt and pepper
egg yolks	

Method

Just simmer the parsley in the chicken stock for about 20 minutes—keep on a slow, quiet roll. When cool put through the blender. At this point, some people strain it but if the blending is done well, why bother? Return to the saucepan and add egg yolks beaten into cream. Now you have to be careful. Stir over very low heat and allow the soup to thicken very slowly—on no account must it come to the boil. Season and serve. The amounts used will naturally vary for the number to be fed. Two egg yolks to 3-4 cups stock and 2 cups of parsley and cream will serve 3-4 people.

Chopped parsley beaten into butter and put into individual serve-size pots and then chilled makes a nice addition to the table for serving with root vegetables. Maitre d'hotel butter for use with steaks is made by adding a little lemon juice to the parsley butter. Cream or cottage cheese is more nutritious when parsley is added.

TABOULEH

Ingredients

1 cup bulgur (cracked wheat)	3 tablespoons lemon juice
2 cups cold water	½ cup finely chopped chives or spring onions
3 cups finely chopped parsley	¼ cup olive oil
salt and pepper	

Method

Soak the bulgur in the water for an hour. Drain, pressing well to get out as much water as possible and spread out on a large plate while chopping the parsley, stalks and all, and the onions and the mint.

Add the green herbs to the bulgur. Mix the olive oil with the lemon juice and season well and stir into the mixture.

As further ingredients, you can also add a generous quantity chopped mint and 2 skinned chopped tomatoes. I find tabouleh keeps better if the tomatoes are added just before serving.

If you find you like more oil and lemon juice this can be added later. This may not be the classic dish, but it always goes down well.

MEDICINAL USE: Stomachic, diuretic, expectorant, emmenogoguic, antiseptic.

Parsley tea will aid digestion and ease kidney and bladder complaints; it is also good for rheumatic conditions and the cramps that can accompany menstruation.

Parsley contains apiol which increases the circulation of the blood in the pelvic organs and if use is made of the seeds, it should be moderate—pregnant women should be particularly careful.

The bruised leaves and stems can be applied fresh to wounds and insect bites. The chewed leaves will sweeten the breath, particularly after garlic has been eaten.

COSMETIC USE

Chopped parsley soaked in boiling water and left until cool can be used as a face-poultice for acne. Just press the warm leaves on the skin and lie down for a time. The water makes a cleansing wash or shampoo.

IN THE GARDEN

Aphids don't like parsley, so a border of it makes a good protection for your vegetables. It is said to improve the taste of both fruit and vegetables and to increase the scent of roses. Bees love it.

The best argument I know for the growing of parsley is its use in the making of tabouleh, that magnificent Middle Eastern dish which must be among the most health-giving possible. If you become a tabouleh addict, you will need great beds of parsley.

PARSLEY PIERT — Breakstone

Botanical name: *Alchemilla arvensis*
Family: *Rosaceae*
Part used: Herb

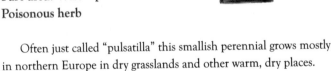

Parsley piert grows wild on stony barren ground in northern latitudes and is a small plant with small, deeply-lobed pale leaves that are lightly hairy and tiny yellow flowers which grow in clusters. It can be introduced to a suitable spot in the garden.

MEDICINAL USE: Demulcent, diuretic.

A tea made from the leaves will promote the flow of urine and is useful in all kidney and bladder complaints particularly where gravel is present, hence the country name "breakstone." Many herbalists regard it as a sovereign remedy. The dried herb can be bought commercially.

PASQUE FLOWER — Meadow Anemone, Easter Flower, Wind Flower

Botanical name: *Pulsatilla vulgaris*
Family: *Ranunculaceae*
Part used: Whole plant
Poisonous herb

Often just called "pulsatilla" this smallish perennial grows mostly in northern Europe in dry grasslands and other warm, dry places. The flowers are beautiful, bell-shaped and rich purple with prominent yellow stamens. The leaves are thin and hairy as are the stems and touching them can irritate the skin quite badly.

The fresh herb is said to be poisonous.

MEDICINAL USE: Sedative, diaphoretic, diuretic, alterative.

Conventional medicine no longer makes use of this plant, but it makes a valuable homoeopathic remedy much used for the weepy type of nervous exhaustion and can be useful in cases of pre-menstrual tension and migraine. It has a beneficial effect on the mucous membranes.

PENNYROYAL — Pudding Grass, Hysteric Grass, Flea Mint, Squaw Mint

Botanical name: *Mentha pulegium* (**European pennyroyal**), *Hedeoma pulegiodes* (**American pennyroyal**)
Part used: Whole plant

The European pennyroyal is a low-growing creeping plant with small oval leaves that can be slightly hairy and tiny lavender-colored flowers in axillary whorls. The American variety grows upright to about 10 inches (25cm) and has sharply pointed leaves and pale blue flowers; it likes a sandy soil in full sun, whereas the European variety prefers a heavy moist soil and protection from full sun. Both plants have the same properties and can make useful garden flowers; the European variety looks pretty in a hanging basket.

CULINARY USE

If you are temporarily without mint, use a few pennyroyal leaves instead—the flavor is similar but more pungent.

MEDICINAL USE: Sudorific, sedative, carminative, stimulant, diaphoretic, emmenogoguic.

A tea made from the plant is excellent for sudden chills and fevers as it will promote a healthy sweat and is particularly useful when menstruation is delayed due to exposure to cold— or for any other reason. The strong peppermint flavor is pleasant and a hot drink of the tea can soothe an upset stomach and take away nausea, calm the nerves and loosen phlegm on the chest—it is also good for children suffering from whooping cough. It is not good for pregnant women, as it stimulates the uterus. The tea can be made using both the green plant and the roots (1oz/30g plant to 22 cups/600mL boiling water) and should be taken in large cupful doses twice a day. Try pennyroyal tea for cramps.

If you dislike bought insect repellents try rubbing a few fresh leaves over exposed skin when midges and mosquitoes are about; you can also rub it into your pet's fur to keep fleas away and tuck some flesh leaves into their sleeping blankets.

DOMESTIC USE

Keep a few sprigs of pennyroyal on the pantry shelves to deter ants. In the garden, pennyroyal will also keep ants at bay. The creeping plant makes a pretty ground cover near vegetables.

The dried flowers and leaves give color and scent to potpourri.

PEPPER

Botanical name: *Piper nigrum*
Family: *Piperaceae*
Part used: Berries

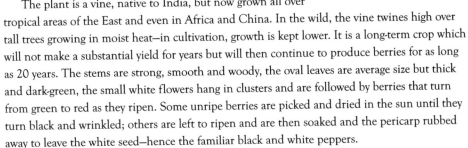

It is strange to realize that pepper, which we now take for granted as part of our lives, was once a reason for the rise and fall of trading empires and that men died in the struggle to control its distribution.

The plant is a vine, native to India, but now grown all over tropical areas of the East and even in Africa and China. In the wild, the vine twines high over tall trees growing in moist heat—in cultivation, growth is kept lower. It is a long-term crop which will not make a substantial yield for years but will then continue to produce berries for as long as 20 years. The stems are strong, smooth and woody, the oval leaves are average size but thick and dark-green, the small white flowers hang in clusters and are followed by berries that turn from green to red as they ripen. Some unripe berries are picked and dried in the sun until they turn black and wrinkled; others are left to ripen and are then soaked and the pericarp rubbed away to leave the white seed—hence the familiar black and white peppers.

Less well known are the green peppercorns that are picked unripe and pickled when fresh.

CULINARY USE

Both black and white peppers can be bought whole or ground; black have the stronger flavor. The whole peppers are added to pickles, etc., and the ground ones used to flavor savory dishes, salads and vegetables. Whole bruised peppers can be pressed into meat to make "pepper steaks." An apple pie can be given a whole new flavor by the addition of some freshly ground black pepper.

MEDICINAL USE: Carminative, stimulant, bacterial.

By encouraging the flow of gastric juices, pepper aids digestion and relieves stomach wind; if a dish is rich and likely to cause trouble, add plenty of pepper. Grind pepper over meat that is likely to be left in the refrigerator for a few days to keep it fresh.

PERIWINKLE — Joy of the Ground

Botanical name: *Vinca major*, *Vinca minor*
Part used: Leaves

Both large and small varieties of this plant are evergreen with clean, shiny leaves and clear blue flowers. The smooth stems grow low over the ground and the plants make an excellent cover for a bank or difficult corner as well as elsewhere in the garden for they are quite good-tempered about soil and shade.

MEDICINAL USE: Astringent, tonic, vulnerary.

The leaves are astringent and can dry internal or external hemorrhage, ease diarrhea and indigestion and act as a tonic. A weak tea made from the leaves should be taken in no more than wineglassful doses as an overdose can cause real upset.

You may find periwinkle ointment on sale—it is good for skin inflammation and small sores. *Vinca rosea*—a South African plant with pinkish-white flowers—is said to be more effective than insulin in the treatment of diabetes.

PLANTAIN – Ripple Grass, Waybread, Rat's Tail

Botanical name: *Plantago major*
Family: *Plantaginaceae*
Part used: Leaves

This perennial has found its way around most of the temperate areas of the world and doubtless one of the family, of which there are several species, has found its way into your lawn. Plantago major is the largest family member, growing to about 12 feet (0.5m) high with large, oval, heavily-veined leaves growing in a rosette at the base of the plant and a long spike of tiny greenish-pink flowers. Though it has no looks, it is a splendid medicinal herb so when you find a plantain, do use it.

MEDICINAL USE: Cooling, alterative, diuretic, emmenogoguic, astringent, de-obstruent, styptic, vulnerary.

The fresh leaves pressed on a wound will stop the bleeding and rubbed on the skin are as effective as dock for easing nettle stings and will take away the itch of insect bites. If you have a sting that looks infected, make a hot poultice of the bruised leaves; this is also good for a stubborn boil or nasty carbuncle, or when sufficiently cool can be used as an external application for inflamed piles, burns and scalds. A gentle enema made from a tea of a few freshly chopped leaves to a cup of boiling water can be used when the bowels are empty and the infusion is cool, will ease the pain of piles. A weak tea, drunk regularly, will rid the body of excess moisture; a stronger one is useful in cases of intermittent fever, asthma, worms. The weak tea also makes a good eye wash but is better made with distilled water, so it is said.

Since plantain is a de-obstruent, it should be considered for use when the sinuses are blocked.

POKE ROOT – Pigeon Berry, Virginia Poke

Botanical name: *Phytolacca decandra*
Family: *Phytolaccaceae*
Parts used: Leaves, roots and berries
Poisonous herb

This North American native shrubby perennial has pale green leaves, pale flowers and purple berries. It is said the leaves can be eaten when young and that the root makes a good spring tonic—on the other hand, the whole plant grows toxic as it ages, so care must obviously be taken.

MEDICINAL USE: Emetic, cathartic, alterative, detergent, antiscorbutic, de-obstruent.

The root has a powerful effect on the glandular system and is an excellent medicine for the renewal and revival of tissues so that their ability to carry out their functions is improved. The fresh root is particularly good for disorders of the thyroid gland and enlargement of the spleen. As an external poultice it is good for rheumatism and inflammations and a tea makes a good skin-wash in cases of eczema or impetigo, scabies, etc. The powdered root is sold as a purgative. The berries have much the same functions as the root, but are gentler in action. Any medication taken internally should be under professional supervision.

POPPY

Botanical name: *Papaver*
Family: *P. somniferum*
Parts used: Pods and seeds

The best known of the family is the opium poppy, a native of the East, but which will grow in more temperate parts of the world given a moist soil and plenty of sunshine. It is a tall annual plant with bluish-green stems, coarse toothed leaves and whitish-blue flowers with a purple mark at the base. The seedpods are round to oval, white or a darkish gray; the seeds are numerous and gray. This is the toxic poppy, a plant that has to be understood. The seedpods are the source of the opium, which provides morphine, heroin and codeine; the seeds themselves are not said to be toxic at all. *P. somniferum* is widely considered to be the only member of the family which has opium in its sap.

P. orientalis, a much more showy species, is a perennial which grows to about 3 feet (1m) high, with the typical leaves and large flower-heads which can be single or double and range in color through red and orange to shades of pink. It likes a reasonably cool climate, an open soil that will not puddle and gentle sun.

It can be propagated from seed or by root division.

P. rhoeas, the corn poppy, is commonly found growing wild among fields of corn. Some varieties have small-lobed leaves, others larger ones—all have the well-known red flowers with a dark spot at the base.

CULINARY USE

Poppy seeds are used in the making of bread and cakes and are sprinkled on bread rolls and pastries, etc. The crushed seeds can be added to curry dishes or, lightly roasted, to the little pats of butter served with steaks.

MEDICINAL USE

A tea made from the seeds is gently soporific and will soothe jangled nerves and go some way toward easing the pain of toothache, earache, etc.

If you grow *P. somniferum* no attempt should be made to make use of it medicinally—its properties are ones which should only be prepared and prescribed under the strictest professional supervision.

PURSLANE

Botanical name: *Portulaca oleracea*
Family: *Portulacaceae*
Parts used: Leaves and stems

Purslane grows wild in the Middle East and India and is cultivated in many parts of the Western world. It is a low-growing annual with fleshy stems and small thick leaves growing in a rosette and pretty greenish flowers with long stamens.

It likes heat, rich soil and plenty of water and grows well from seed. The yellow-flowered variety, *P. oleracea sativa*, is very susceptible to frost.

CULINARY USE

The young leaves can be cooked as a vegetable or used in a salad—they have a light, sharp, cool taste. Try a bundle of young shoots cooked as for asparagus.

MEDICINAL USE: Cooling, tonic.

Tea made from the leaves will help in feverish conditions—they can be used either fresh or dried. It was once used against scurvy so it follows that it must also be a supplier of Vitamin C.

QUASSIA – Bitter Ash

Botanical name: *Picraena excelsa*
Part used: Bark

It may seem strange to think of so tall a tree with so thick a trunk as an herb.

It is included because of the use made of the bark. It is native to the West Indies and Central America, and has a smooth, gray bark and yellow flowers.

MEDICINAL USE: Tonic

The bark chips, which can be bought from an herbalist, can be steeped in water to give a bitter drink that will stimulate the appetite and digestive ability.

There is no point in pretending it tastes nice, but desperate dyspeptics, for whom nothing else has worked, could give it a go.

IN THE GARDEN

One of the best garden sprays against caterpillars and aphids is made from quassia chips. The best part about it is that the ladybirds that live on the aphids and do good to the garden will be unaffected.

RASPBERRY

Botanical name: *Rubus idaeus*
Species: *R. strigosus*
Parts used: Fruit and leaves

The raspberry is included because the wild variety was so esteemed by early herbalists for the use made of its leaves. It is a native of the northern hemisphere and will only grow well in the parts of the southern hemisphere that can offer a coolish summer. If you are determined to try it, despite local summer heat, give the canes a shaded spot and be prepared to keep up their moisture supply. The soil should be a rich loam, and the plants will need support; short poles with wire running between them will do.

The canes should be planted about 3 feet (1m) apart with 3 feet (1m) between the rows.

They will give fruit after two years and then will die as new young shoots push up and will then need cutting out.

CULINARY USE

To many people the raspberry is the queen of fruits, surpassing the strawberry for taste. Since the fruit is rich in Vitamin C, iron and Vitamin B elements, it makes an excellent food and drink. It is delicious served fresh or lightly stewed and then covered with yogurt sprinkled with raw sugar before taking to the table. Surplus crop can be frozen in the comfortable knowledge that most of the nutritives will be preserved.

RASPBERRY JAM

Using about 1½ pounds (750g) berries to 1 pound (500g) sugar, stir the mixture over low heat until all the sugar is dissolved and then bring it up to the boil and maintain it there for at least 20 minutes or until a drop of the jam will jell when dropped into cold water or on to a plate just taken from the refrigerator. A little grated lemon rind adds to the flavor. Have ready some hot, sterilized jars, pour the jam in, cover and seal when cool.

Mrs. Beeton, a famous English homemaker, probably mindful of the little pips, gives a recipe for raspberry jelly made by crushing the fruit well during gentle heating and then straining it when sufficient juice has been extracted, before boiling up a mixture of 1 pound (450g) sugar to 2½ cups (600mL) juice until setting point is reached.

The most can be made of the fruit by serving them frosted. The method is simple. Just beat up a white of egg in a little water, dip the fruit in and cover well, drain and then roll in caster sugar and spread out to dry on waxed paper for about 4 hours in a warm spot.

A drink packed full of Vitamin C is made by liquifying a small cucumber, straining it then adding the liquid to 2 cups raspberry juice, 1 cup orange juice and 1 cup lemon juice. Sweeten with honey and reduce with water to taste and serve chilled.

A raspberry vinegar for enlivening stewed fruit used in pies and puddings is made by steeping the fruit in wine vinegar for a week or more, stirring occasionally with a wooden, not metal, spoon. Strain to obtain the juice, and using about 1 pound (400g) sugar to 2½ cups (600mL) liquid, heat gently until the sugar is dissolved before boiling up and keeping at the boil for at least 10 minutes. Be certain to skim off the scum before carefully pouring into hot, sterilized bottles. Seal when cool.

Only a touch of this vinegar is needed for flavoring. It is particularly good with pears.

MEDICINAL USE: Astringent, stimulant, sudorific, tonic.

The raspberry vinegar described above can be used medicinally; taken in hot water it is good for chills and fever, stomach upset, vomiting and as a gargle for a sore throat. Olive oil, made palatable by the addition of raspberry vinegar, can be sipped and allowed to go down the throat slowly to ease any soreness. The raspberry appears to contain a water-soluble substance, fragrine, which has a soothing effect on mucous membranes. A tea made from the leaves will ease diarrhea and painful menstruation and since it acts as a tonic to the reproductive organs is often recommended for pregnant women.

COSMETIC USE

A tea made from the leaves makes a mild astringent face wash.

IN THE GARDEN

Do not grow raspberry canes near potatoes or the potatoes will become more susceptible to blight.

RED CLOVER — Bee Bread, Clavers

Botanical name: *Trifolium pratense*
Family: *Leguminosae*
Parts used: Leaves and flowers

Clover grows wild in grassland in temperate regions, covering the ground in a clump that can grow as much as 24 inches (60cm) high. The leaves are a strong green and grow in threes at the end of a slender stem—to find a four-leaved clover is said to be lucky. The pinky-purple flowers grow in a head of pea-type blossoms and make a mildly fragrant "ball." Country children pull them apart and suck out the sweetness. The roots manufacture nitrogen so, if you find clover in the lawn, carefully dig it out and add the whole plant to the compost.

MEDICINAL USE: Alterative, sedative, depurative.

A tea made from the leaves and flowers (1 ounce/30g to 2½ cups/600mL boiling water) makes, a pleasant drink when flavored with lemon juice and honey and, taken regularly, keeps the nerves steady and is good for the digestion. It is a good simple remedy for whooping cough and also a splendid blood purifier. Poisons left in the body after prolonged drug treatment can be eliminated by drinking plenty of clover tea. There is a strong case for its efficacy, against tumors, internal and external. Violet leaves, which have the same ability, can be used with the clover blossom in the making of an ointment for external use—violet flowers are often included too. All are boiled together until reduced to a thick dark paste. Try this for obstinate cases of athlete's foot too.

It is well worthwhile trying a douche of clover tea in cases of uterine cancer. After douching, lie down quietly for about half an hour to keep the warm liquid in the vagina.

COSMETIC USE

A face wash of clover tea is good for dry skin and will ease the itch of eczema.

RHUBARB

Botanical name: *Rheum palmatum*
Species: *R. officinale*, *R. rhubarbarum*
Parts used: Rhizomes (roots) and stem. Never use the leaves—they are toxic

Rheum palmatum—often known as Turkey rhubarb—is a native of China and got its name because it reached Europe through the port of Constantinople, among others. In the East it was used medicinally for thousands of years before Christ.

In appearance, it is very like the garden rhubarb with which we are all familiar but the leaves are more heavily cut. Bought medicines are likely to have been made from Turkey rhubarb.

The garden rhubarb requires a lightish but well-fed and well-drained soil; you will never get a good crop if the soil is heavy and holds water. The rhizomes should not be deeply planted and should be given at least 20 inches (50cm) space all round.

The plants can be "forced" to give an early crop by surrounding each one by some sort of open-ended protection and packing fresh manure around the base. It is hardly worth doing this in other than areas with a chilly spring as the leaves on their strong reddish-green "sticks" or petioles are forceful growers in gentle warmth. Once the plant is established, it can be easily divided by splitting off the outer root sections with a spade and replanting them in the autumn.

CULINARY USE

The "sticks" are used to make stewed fruit, jam and wine. The nutritional value is surprisingly high as iron, potassium and several vitamins and minerals are present.

Rhubarb and apple jam made by using twice the amount of apple to rhubarb is an old favorite. Use 2 pounds (1kg) sugar to 2 pounds (1kg) apples and 1 pound (0.5kg) rhubarb and make in the usual way. A little lemon juice gives added flavor. This is not a jam which "jells" readily, but do not be alarmed, it will set in the jar.

A clean-tasting, nicely sharp jam is made using lemon-juice and ginger—preferably the root. The Mrs. Beeton recipe is excellent.

RHUBARB AND GINGER JAM

Ingredients

3½ pounds (1.5kg) rhubarb

3½ pounds (1.5kg) sugar

juice of 3 lemons (some finely grated peel can be added too)

1 ounce (30g) ginger root

Method

Cut up the rhubarb into small pieces and layer with the sugar in a glass dish and then pour the lemon juice evenly over the mixture and leave to stand, covered, overnight. Next day, bruise the ginger root well and tie up in thin cloth and place with the rhubarb etc in an enameled saucepan—on no account use an aluminum one. Bring to the boil and keep there until the jam falls in flakes from a wooden spoon or, when dropped onto a cold plate, will set and wrinkle as it cools.

RHUBARB WINE

This wine is delightfully potent but is best left to the aficionados who will take the trouble to learn how to deal with the oxalic acid the stems contain before embarking on the enterprise.

A red or white wine can be made into a good tonic by adding rhubarb, gentian and angelica root in the proportion of 4 cups (1L) wine to 2 ounces (60g) bruised rhubarb root, ½ ounce (15g) bruised gentian root and ⅓ ounce (10g) bruised angelica root. Leave the liquid to steep for at least 2 days and then strain well. Wineglassful doses will act as a tonic, larger doses as a splendid relief for stubborn constipation.

MEDICINAL USE: Astringent, tonic, stomachic, aperient.

Turkey rhubarb is the strongest in effect.

The root of the garden rhubarb can be cut into pieces, dried slowly until it can be reduced to a powder. A little powder taken with honey or jam will enable stubborn bowels to move without griping as it will help the muscles to act of their own accord. The liver will also be helped to get rid of bile. In smaller doses it acts the opposite way and will regulate loose bowels.

COSMETIC USE

Powdered rhubarb root can be mixed to a paste and combed through the hair to make it lighter.

HOUSEHOLD USE

Give very dirty brass or copper articles a good rub over with rhubarb leaves before using a commercial cleaner. Rinse off and dry well before proceeding.

Boil up any part of the plant in a kettle that has become "scaly." You may have to do it several times but the oxalic acid in the plant will finally render the utensil clean.

ROSEMARY — Dew of the Sea

Botanical name: *Rosmarinus officinalis*
Family: *Laciatae*
Parts used: Leaves and flowers

Rosemary—*rosmarinus*—Latin for "dew of the sea"—is a shrubby aromatic plant that grows well near salt water but is also found in the Sahara Desert. It is a plant no garden should be without, not only for the pleasure of its presence but for the manifold uses to which it can be put.

The shrub has thin, dark-green leaves, silver on the underside, highly aromatic; the flowers, much beloved of bees, are small, mauve-blue, and grow along the stems as well as at the tips. Like the lavender, rosemary can be trained to make a hedge as the stems become woody and strong. It likes a light and well-drained soil. Propagation is easy. The plant will layer and grow from either root division or heeled cuttings—it is hardly worthwhile taking the time to grow it from the seed although that is quite easy too and some people think the best plants are produced this way. There is a white variety and a low-growing sprawling one, which is smaller and rather more delicate and needs more water than the larger one, which, as a native of the dry rocks of the Mediterranean area, can take a certain amount of drought. Once established, all the plants are long-living.

CULINARY USE

The leaves, used either fresh or dried, are good with meat dishes, particularly lamb. The flavor is strong so they should always be used sparingly.

A pinch of the dried herb will be sufficient added to stews or casseroles and sauces—any fresh leaves rubbed over meat should be taken out before serving. Roast duck and pork, both rich dishes, benefit by a touch of rosemary. Soak a sprig of rosemary in the milk used for making puddings or custard; burn a few sprigs on the barbecue to give sausages and chops a good flavor; keep a jar of sugar containing rosemary sprigs to make a final sprinkling over fruit pies. The flowers can be frosted by dipping in white of egg and fine sugar and then left to dry and used as an edible garnish for cakes or salads.

MEDICINAL USE: Tonic, astringent, diuretic, nervine, antispasmodic, stimulant, carminative, antiseptic, emmenogoguic and possibly abortive.

The valuable oil made from rosemary is liable to be expensive as the yield is low; it is excellent as a rub for painful rheumatic joints, a wound disinfectant and as a scalp tonic when hair is beginning to fall out. Many bought shampoos and hair tonics contain rosemary in some form. A tea made from the flowering tops is good for strained nerves, bad headaches and retention of urine and bile; in stronger concentration it will aid the expulsion of worms, but should be used with care as strong doses can be both toxic and abortive. It is said that if the flowering tops are steeped in white wine for a week the strained liquid, taken in smallish doses, will not only aid a failing memory but will clear dim eyesight and ease palpitation of the heart. If you have a bad cold or are troubled by blocked sinus, try covering the head with a towel and leaning over a bowl of boiling water containing a handful of fresh rosemary leaves while you take in deep breaths keeping the mouth as closed as possible. And if you are plagued by troubled sleep and nightmares, nothing will be lost by slipping a few sprigs of the flowering plant into your pillowslip as people in medieval times used to do.

COSMETIC USE

Rosemary tea makes a good hair- and face-rinse. A stronger hair tonic is made by simmering the leaves for at least half an hour before use. This is not only good for dandruff but gives a strong, clean fragrance to the hair. The weaker tea, used carefully only once a day, will reduce eye-puffiness. Pat on very gently.

HOUSEHOLD USE

Mosquitoes do not like the scent of rosemary; rub a few leaves on the skin when they are about. Moths don't like it either, particularly when used with tansy, mint and thyme. The dried herbs can be powdered and sewn into little bags for hanging in the wardrobe or tucking between wool clothing in a drawer.

IN THE GARDEN

Cabbage worm butterflies do not like the scent of rosemary, so keep a few plants nearby; however potatoes will not grow well if rosemary is in the vicinity. Sage, on the other hand, grows better and has a stronger taste if it is grown near rosemary in the herb garden.

RUE — Herb of Grace, Herb of Repentance

Botanical name: *Ruta graveolens*
Family: *Rutaceae*
Part used: Herb

Rue is a dainty plant, growing to about 3 feet (1m) high with feathery blue-green leaves and pretty yellow flowers. It makes a good garden border as it is almost evergreen.

Rue is a plant you have to learn about for it has its good and bad sides. It will take a poor soil and die off if fed too well; needs the right amount of sun; it is lovely as a vase flower—if you can pick it without feeling skin irritation in the handling.

If you grow it near sage or basil, it will poison them, but it will keep away slugs and other insects from surrounding plants. It did not earn the name "herb of grace" for nothing—you just have to understand it.

CULINARY USE

Nibble a leaf. If you like the flavor it can be used in salads and sandwiches.

MEDICINAL USE

Anthelmintic, antispasmodic, stimulant, emmenogoguic.

The flowers contain a substance that can prevent the formation of cataract, so a mild tea made from them makes a good eye bath. Both Michelangelo and Leonardo are said to have used it. An infusion made with 1 ounce (30g) plant to 22 cups (600mL) water taken in cupful doses is good for flatulence, colic, nervous upset, and painful and suppressed menstruation due to congestion of the uterus. It will also help to expel worms from the body. In the old days the seeds, steeped in wine, were a well-known remedy for the stings of serpents, scorpions and poisonous flying insects and were part of the medicines used when plagues were raging. Rue was a "strewing herb" to keep down fleas and flies so a few sprigs in kennel and larder are worth a try. Rutin, one of the best substances known for strengthening the blood vessels, is obtained from rue—you can buy rutin commercially as a remedy for high blood-pressure; if you have rue in the garden, why not use the leaves to make a tea?

You are unlikely to overdose with it as the flavor, though aromatic, is bitter. An overdose can cause an upset of the stomach and, possibly, abortion.

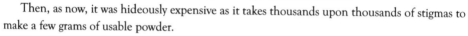

SAFFRON — Alicante Crocus, Valencia Crocus
Botanical name: *Crocus sativus*
Family: *Iridaceae*
Part used: Flower stigmas

A native of the eastern Mediterranean, saffron, once introduced into Spain, became regarded as more Spanish than Greek or Persian; cultivation even penetrated as far as England, where, in the reign of Henry VIII, ladies of the court used the yellow stigmas to dye their hair blonde.

Then, as now, it was hideously expensive as it takes thousands upon thousands of stigmas to make a few grams of usable powder.

The plant grows from a corm and the bluish-purple flowers are very like those of the ordinary crocus but have 3 very large reddish-gold stigmas protruding from the flower. If you can obtain the corms, you will not find them difficult to grow provided the soil is light and sandy and the weather is mild. Propagation can be made by splitting the corm mass and replanting the small new ones.

When the flower is in full bloom the stigmas can be nipped off for drying. This is worth doing even if you only have a few flowers, as the merest pinch will give color to rice dishes, cakes, paella and the great French fish soup, bouillabaisse. It is no good pretending you can make true bouillabaisse anywhere but on the French Mediterranean shores, but that has never stopped cooks from trying.

CULINARY USE

FISH SOUP

You will need at least 8 kinds of fish and will need to know which have firm flesh and which have soft flesh. This is not a dish to be undertaken lightly. Sort out your fish, cut them up small and keep separate after weighing. For a dinner-party for 8 people you will need 2 pounds (1kg) fish.

For each 2 pounds (1kg) of fish you will need

Ingredients

2 large onions   some chopped parsley with an addition of tarragon or fennel

| 2 tomatoes | a good pinch saffron |
| 1 clove garlic | 1 bay leaf |

Method

Place chopped onions, sliced, skinned tomatoes and the crushed garlic, evenly and carefully distributed, on the base of a large dish and cover with the pieces of firm-fleshed fish. Season with the salt and pepper, add saffron and herbs, the olive oil and then the white wine or white vinegar. If this does not cover the fish add a little water. Place the dish in a hot oven and bring the liquid to the boil and keep it there for at least 7-8 minutes. If you are using a microwave oven, the time will naturally be less. Add the rest of the fish, pressing down into the liquid and bring back to the boil. Keep it there for 5 minutes in a conventional oven, 2-3 in a microwave one.

This makes a very thick soup that will need a fork as well as a spoon to eat.

It can be poured over *croutons* of toasted or fried bread as it is, or the liquid can be poured over the bread and the fish eaten separately. The saffron will take care of the color, the seasoning is up to the cook. If you like garlic, fry your *croutons* in oil in which garlic cloves have been macerating. It may be heresy but the best bouillabaisse I ever had contained a strong dash of something between chili and mustard. This is clearly a dish that can be all things to all men, so use your own ingenuity in the seasoning. Saffron has an elusive flavor—a pinch can be just right, two pinches can be all wrong. You won't need more than a quarter-teaspoon when making paella—a very large paella too. Paella is of course a traditionally Spanish dish made with a mixture of chicken and seafood served with rice cooked in stock, with a liberal lacing of garlic and peppers added too. At its simplest all you do is to add onions, peppers and tomatoes which have been sautéed in oil and garlic and then boiled up with water, plenty of seasoning and that touch of saffron to cooked rice and small bite-sized pieces of cooked chicken, prawns, scallops and mussels which you then cook together for a few minutes for the flavors to blend.

Paella is a splendidly informal dish; saffron gives it a wonderful color and you may be able to detect its lightly pungent taste among all the others. Saffron can be used to color and flavor any cake but the traditional one, which can be a bit tiresome to make, is well worth a try. It uses yeast.

SAFFRON CAKE

Ingredients

1 pound (450g) plain flour	½ ounce (15g) yeast
7 ounces (200g) margarine	1¼ (300mL) warm water
salt	4½ ounces (125g) sugar
4½ ounces (125g) dried fruit	a large pinch saffron powder
2 eggs	

Method

Cream the yeast in a little of the warm water, carefully add the sifted flour and knead into a soft dough using as much of the water as is necessary. Leave in a warm place until it is seen the dough is rising well then add the chopped margarine, sugar, beaten eggs and fruit and knead again, carefully adding the saffron which has been soaking in the rest of the water. Some people strain it. Leave the well-kneaded dough to rise, and don't be impatient. Bake in loaf tins—2 will be enough for this amount—for about 90 minutes at 375°F or 180°C.

When this cake comes off, it is splendid; I have never worked out why it can sometimes be such a failure.

MEDICINAL USE: Sedative, emmenogoguic.

Saffron is a powerful drug which, used indiscreetly, can cause hemorrhage, but in moderate use, a light pinch of powder to a glass of hot water will ease stomach upset and bring on perspiration and menstruation. Conversely it will arrest uterine bleeding, so it is obvious that saffron should be used, as a drug, under expert guidance, but since its use has largely been superseded, that guidance may be hard to find.

Saffron is not only expensive to buy but, even when you find it, it could be adulterated by the addition of dried petals of the same bright color, so is an herb to approach with circumspection.

SAGE

Botanical name: *Salvia officinalis*
Family: *Labiateae*
Part used: Leaves

Sage is a perennial, rather bushy plant with gray-green leaves, smooth on the top surface and rough on the underside, and with a wrinkled feel. The flowers are usually purplish or blue though different varieties can have red, white or pink flowers. A native of the northern shores of the Mediterranean, its cultivation has spread around the world and there are many different varieties.

Sage will grow in most climates given a sunny position and well-drained soil; it will tolerate some lime. Propagation is best done by cuttings or layering.

CULINARY USE

The leaves, which can be used either fresh or dried, have a strong, clean flavor that cuts the grease of fatty foods and so makes it popular in stuffings for pork or goose and with sausages. Its flavor combines particularly well with onion. The chopped fresh leaves make a good addition to homemade yogurt and sour-milk cheese, stews, casseroles, etc. Chopped well, it can make a cheese sandwich into something special. Sage cheese is a regional speciality in England.

MEDICINAL USE: Digestive, tonic, nervine, anti-inflammatory, oestrogenic.

Sage tea is recommended for nervous disorders and depression and for drying up the milk of nursing mothers. The plant contains estrogen and can therefore tone up the female reproductive organs. It will also clean out mucus from the digestive and respiratory tracts. A decoction of sage leaves (½ ounce/15g leaves to 4 cups/1L of water) boiled up and left to stand until cool makes a good mouthwash for inflamed gums, mouth ulcers and tooth abscesses as well as a gargle for a sore throat, and the boiled leaves, made into a poultice, will both ease and heal painful wounds and suppurating boils, etc. Asthma sufferers should try smoking the dried leaves instead of tobacco.

COSMETIC USE

Sage tea makes a good hair tonic If your hair is beginning to turn gray, use it as a final rinse, stronger for brunettes than blondes. If body odor persists despite the use of bought deodorants, make a habit of chewing a few sage leaves each day—this will also help to keep the teeth white. If you have forgotten to buy toothpaste or don't have a toothbrush handy, give the teeth a good rub over with fresh sage leaves.

HOUSEHOLD USE

Moths don't like sage so keep sachets of the dried leaves in the wardrobe or between wool clothing stored away for the summer.

IN THE GARDEN

Dried sage sprinkled around plants will help to keep them free from mildew. The carrot-fly and the cabbage moth detest the smell, so either grow a few plants nearby or sprinkle the dried powder between the rows and around the plants. Incidentally, sage should always be dried very slowly—if you rush it, the leaves will turn brown and, when stored, soon develop a nasty musty odor. Only use dried sage that has kept its strong green color.

ST JOHN'S WORT — Klamath Weed
Botanical name: *Hypericum perforatum*
Family: *Hypericaceae*
Part used: Herb

The plant grows wild in Europe and Asia and is a small perennial with reddish-tinged stems, small oval leaves which look dark because of the oil glands which dot them and 5-petalled flowers, a sunny golden color with prominent dark stamens. If these flowers are squeezed, they exude a dark-red oil.

MEDICINAL USE: Astringent, expectorant, diuretic, sedative.

A tea made from the dried leaves and flowers is good for coughs, colds and all lung complaints and will ease painful micturition. It is also good for the liver and acts as a mild sedative. To make a simple massage oil for painful joints and sprains, soak fresh flowers in olive oil for a month. Use strained. This oil also makes a dressing for wounds, ulcers and burns.

SALAD BURNET

Botanical name: *Poterium sanguisoba*
Family: *Rosaceae*
Part used: Leaves

This pretty low-growing perennial with its lacy leaves and tiny greenish-red flowers makes a lovely bushy border plant for the main garden as well as the herb plot. It likes a light soil with full sun but plenty of moisture. Since it will self-sow and also keep its leaves for most of the winter it is more than ordinarily useful. If you wish to space out the seedlings do it while they are small—larger plants resent disturbance.

CULINARY USE

Since this plant does not dry well and the leaves are best used fresh, a pot on the kitchen windowsill should be considered. The leaves have a light cucumber-like taste and when chopped, make a tasty addition to salads, cream cheese and cottage cheese, fruit drinks and herb butters. Steeped in wine vinegar they will keep for use in making French dressing.

Some people also use them in soups and casseroles but the delicate flavor tends to become lost; however, since they can help to prevent an upset stomach, if you have them why not use them? Should the plants threaten to die off, a few sprigs can be wrapped in foil and stored in the freezing compartment of the refrigerator.

MEDICINAL USE: Tonic, carminative.

Tea made from the leaves tastes fresh and pleasant and acts as a tonic and a stomach "settler."

COSMETIC USE

The pain of sunburn can be eased by bathing the inflamed parts in the tea.

SANTOLINA

Botanical name: *Santolina chamaecyparissus*
Family: *Compositae*
Part used: Leaves

Santolina, a native of the Mediterranean areas, is both good-tempered
and beautiful; it will tolerate a dry spot, make a nice low bush and give color
to the garden. The leaves are silver-gray and grow thickly along the stems and look curiously like
fine coral; the yellow button-shaped flowers lift from the plant on clean tall stems so that dead-
heading is simple and easy.

It can be propagated from cuttings. If the plant spreads more than you like, make any
cutting-back gentle and selective, as it hates hard pruning.

HOUSEHOLD USE

The dried leaves can be used in sachets as a moth-deterrent and added to a potpourri to give
a clean scent. Rubbed to a powder they can be shaken over carpets and left for a time before
vacuuming off; the scent will linger and deter carpet-moths.

IN THE GARDEN

A border of santolina around the rose-bed will help to keep the bushes healthy.

SARSAPARILLA

Botanical name: *Smilax*
Family: *Liliaceae*
Part used: Roots

There are well over 200 members of the family and they all
grow in the temperate and tropical parts of Asia and America.
The root is the most valuable part of the plant.

Jamaican Sarsaparilla (*S. ornata*) is thought to be the most useful to man but *S. aristolochiaefolia*, the American species, is very good too.

MEDICINAL USE: Alterative, pectoral, diaphoretic, sudorific.

Boil 1 ounce (30g) of the root in 2½ cups (600mL) water for half an hour and then left to cool and taken in wineglassful doses, is good for all skin diseases and rheumatism because it will purify the blood so well. It is good as a tonic and general regulator of the system, enabling the body to throw off excess water and mucus. Because it is so excellent a blood purifier it was once considered a specific for syphilis. Today one is most likely to find it as a flavoring for fizzy drinks. Some herbalists may stock the root. It is worth searching for.

SAVORY — Bean Herb

Botanical name: *Satureia hortensis* (**Summer savory**)
Species: *S. montana* (**Winter savory**)
S. repandens (**Low-growing Winter savory**)
Part used: Leaves

Summer savory is an annual plant with tender narrow leaves of brownish-green and tiny flowers from pale pink to lavender. It grows easily from seed in both warm and temperate climates. Because of the weakness of the stems it can be an untidy plant.

Winter savory is a perennial plant with thin small leaves, very dark green as they age and very pale when young and with white or blue flowers. The stems are stronger. The low-growing savory will spread over a bank and cover it with a mass of dark leaves and pure white flowers. This variety is mostly used as a garden plant—the other two have both culinary and medicinal value. All the savories like full sun and a well-drained soil.

CULINARY USE

The leaves have a highly individual taste, both sweetly spicy and sharply peppery—the winter savory has the sharper flavor.

Finely chopped, they add flavor to vegetables and have the ability to bring out the "bean" flavor in any bean dish made from either fresh or dried beans without imposing their own. Summer savory, with its milder taste, is the best bet for beans. At a pinch, savory can be used instead of sage as the flavors are something similar; both greasy meats and any food found hard to digest will be less troublesome served with a discreet amount of powdered leaf used either in the cooking or as a garnish. This is the sort of herb that, once the flavor has been approved, can turn up in almost any savory dish from fish and meat to soups, omelets and stuffings. Don't add too much pepper to any dish to which you have added savory and if, on medical grounds, you are not allowed to use either salt or pepper use a sprinkling of powdered savory leaves instead. The leaves dry easily and well, and wrapped in foil can be stored in the freezer part of the refrigerator.

MEDICINAL USE

Carminative, expectorant.

Though very little used today as a medicinal herb it is well worth trying a pinch or two of powdered leaf in hot water both for a stomach upset and a rattly cough and if you are near a winter savory plant when stung by a bee or wasp, snatch up a few leaves, rub them to release the oil and hold tightly over the sting.

If used soon enough there should be little pain and no swelling. The volatile oil in the leaves will still help even when the part stung has become inflamed and swollen.

IN THE GARDEN

Green beans and onions grow better and remain freer from pests when savory is growing nearby.

SESAME — Benne, Tilseed

Botanical name: *Sesamum orientale*
Parts used: Leaves and seeds

Sesame is an Eastern plant and needs steady heat and full sun to do well. It is a strong-growing annual plant with erect stems, shiny leaves and purplish flowers rather like those of the foxglove and, in the right conditions, can grow to 3 feet (1m) high. If you decide to try to grow it for its seeds, allow at least 8 inches (20cm) between the plants of which you will need a good number as the seed yield is not large.

The pods form inside the flowers and burst open, scattering the seed as soon as they ripen so you have to keep your eye on them and pick them for drying at just the right moment.

CULINARY USE

Oil is extracted from the seeds and sold as a cooking or salad oil. The seeds themselves can be sprinkled on bread and cakes, either plain or roasted, or used as an ingredient in the recipe. Since they are rich in protein, iron and Vitamin B they make an excellent food and are widely used in the Middle East in a paste known as tahini, which can be now bought in most parts of the world in delicatessens and health-food shops.

TAHINI SAUCE

Blend half-cup tahini and 2-3 cloves garlic, either by hand or in a food blender. Crush the cloves first of course and remove the skins.

Gradually add a half-cup lemon juice and a half-cup water, alternately, a little at a time, stirring vigorously as you go until the mixture thickens. The amount of water can be increased if you want a runny sauce. Salt can be added to taste. Good with fish.

HUMMUS

This can be gloriously garlicky if you wish. Two cloves are enough for some people, for others, 4 are not enough. The purist will say the skins should be removed from the chickpeas but if that puts you off as being too fiddly, leave them on.

Soak a cup of chickpeas in water to cover overnight then cook in their water, either in a saucepan on top of the stove or in a microwave oven, until they are nicely tender. Some of the skins will float off and can be removed. Drain the water off. Mash the peas well or sieve carefully, discarding as many skins as possible. When as smooth as makes you content, begin to add half-cup tahini and half-cup lemon juice together with the finely crushed garlic. Take time beating it all together and taste as you go, adding a touch of salt if necessary. If it seems too thick, add a little of the cooking water. The taste is wonderful and any remaining pea skins can be regarded as good roughage. This no doubt is heresy but it does not stop my hummus disappearing at great speed. If you really feel you must remove the skins and present the classic dish, soak the peas overnight and then take a few in your hands and rub them together so that the friction loosens the skins. Drop the handful into water and skim off the floating skins. Continue to do this until all the peas have been separated from the skins, which should then be discarded. The dish can be presented covered with chopped parsley and a dusting of paprika pepper—some people go for cayenne which gives not only color but an additional taste and some pour a little olive oil into the center of the dish. Children love sesame sweeties, which are simplicity itself to make.

SESAME SWEETIES

Add 3 ounces (90g) butter or margarine and 1 cup sugar to a large cup of water and stir the mixture over gentle heat until the sugar has dissolved and you have a smoothish mixture. Then add 1 cup toasted sesame seeds, stir in well then boil up quickly and keep on the boil until a golden-brown.

Quickly spread out on a flat tin that has either been well greased or lined with foil that has been lightly greased. Press flat and mark out into bite sizes.

Leave to cool. Remove from tin when cold and snap into pieces. Store in a tightly closed tin if the family leave any to store. Anything coated with breadcrumbs for frying will taste nicer and be crunchier if some sesame seeds are added to the crumbs. The toasted seed can be added to cream and cottage cheeses, sprinkled over potato salads, soups, etc.

The seeds can be bought, ground, as sesame meal, and anyone who has turned vegetarian should include it in the diet as a protein substitute as well as eating plenty of tahini either as a spread plain or mixed with cooked eggplant on toast.

They will probably need no urging to eat Halva, that devilishly sweet and moreish confection so popular with the Greeks. This is one sweet that can be eaten, in judicious quantity, with a relatively clear conscience—the food value, largely because of the sesame content, is high.

MEDICINAL USE: Laxative, urinary.

An infusion of the fresh leaves will ease bladder and kidney upsets. The oil can be taken as a gentle laxative.

A handful of raw unhulled seeds chewed before bedtime will not only supply the body with calcium and 3 essential fatty acids, but will also give the fiber needed by the bowels if they are to act freely. As a nerve food they will also help to give a good night's sleep.

SCULLCAP — Madweed, Quaker Bonnet

Botanical name: *Scutellartia laterifolia*
Part used: Herb

The plant is clearly a member of the nettle family with its square stems, pointed leaves and bluish helmet-shaped flowers. It grows wild in temperate parts of the world and is one of the best of the medicinal plants discovered for the treatment of nervous disorders.

MEDICINAL USE: Tonic, nervine, antispasmodic.

The herb can be bought in its powdered form or in liquid extract. There is nothing better for hysteria, convulsions, St. Vitus Dance and the terrible nervous spasms brought on by hydrophobia. It is a specific for St. Vitus Dance. Anyone bitten by a dog should seek professional advice and dosage of skullcap.

SENNA

Botanical name: *Cassia marilandica* (**wild senna**)
Species: *C. angustifolia, C. acutifolia, C. senna*
Parts used: Leaves and pods

There can be few people born in the Western world in the early part of the century who, in their childhood, did not make the acquaintance of the senna pod. Steeped in hot water, it was the Friday evening bedtime drink; it kept the bowels open.

The senna plant, of which there are many varieties, grows in the Middle East, India, Egypt and North America. The wild variety, *C. marilandica*, makes a tall, bushy plant almost 7 feet (2m) high with light green leaves growing opposite on the stem and lovely clusters of yellow flowers and papery seedpods.

All varieties resemble each other, the difference lies mainly in the size and shape of the leaves. Senna would presumably grow in any part of the world that could offer it a light, sandy soil, sun and moisture and steady warmth. In a pot it makes quite a good-looking plant and out in the garden a handsome one.

MEDICINAL USE: Laxative, cathartic, vermifuge.

The leaves, taken in infusion, have a griping effect on the bowels and in bought preparations are usually combined with other herbs. The pods, which are gentler in action, are the best ones to use for children and anyone subject to stomach cramp. Present knowledge says that senna should not be taken regularly but only when constipation is chronic. If there is any question of bowel inflammation, it should not be taken at all; pregnant women should not take it either, or people suffering from piles. The tea can help to dislodge threadworms.

SHALLOT

Botanical name: *Allium cepa*
Species: *A. ascalonicum, A. fistulosum*
Family: Liliaceae
Parts used: Leaves and bulbs

The term "shallot" is rather loosely used for these smaller members of the onion family; to some people a shallot is a small thin-skinned onion which grows in a bulb which can be divided into cloves—the flavor is mild and the little onions are mostly used for pickles.

To others, shallots are small white bulblets with long hollow green stems and all parts are edible—Welsh onions, spring onions, tree onions, Egyptian onions, whatever they are called, all are valuable plants to grow.

Allium cepa (the tree onion) can produce green hollow stems up to 3 feet (1m) high with flowers growing from a clump of little bulblets at the top of the stem. The bulblets drop to the earth and produce new plants. Propagation can also be made by splitting up the main bulb. The leaves can be used in salads and cooking, the bulbs in cooking.

Allium fistulosum has a tiny bulb and long green stems, which can remain green for most of the year and can be snipped off and used, rather like chives, or the whole plant can be lifted. It grows well from seed and can be propagated by splitting the bulbs in a clump into separate bulblets and replanting each one. This little perennial is a willing self-perpetuator.

A. ascolonicum is the small pickling onion, the true shallot. They all enjoy full sun and good, well-drained soil.

CULINARY USE PICKLED ONIONS

Ingredients

2 pounds (1kg) shallots

2½ cups (600mL) water (salted)

1¼ cups (300mL) white vinegar (some people use malt vinegar instead)

spices: These can be a matter of individual choice but do include a piece of ginger root

Method

Salt the water—this can be a matter of individual preference—if you reduce the amount too far, there will be a loss in flavor. Soak the peeled onions in the water for a whole day, keeping the bowl cool and covered and the onions submerged. Boil up the vinegar with the chosen spices, hold at the boil for a minute or two and then leave to cool.

Drain and rinse the onions and place carefully in sterilized jars making the most of the space. Pour in the cooled, strained vinegar, tapping the jar to release any trapped air as you go. Leave the minimum of air space at the top and then seal the jars and put them in a dark cupboard and forget them for a couple of months. Restraint will pay off.

BEARNAISE SAUCE

Ingredients

½ cup tarragon vinegar

4 small shallots, chopped fine

black pepper and some salt

4 egg yolks

about 3 ounces (80g) butter (margarine if you must, but you'll regret it)

Method

Boil up the seasoned tarragon vinegar with the chopped shallots, reduce to a simmer and hold until the shallots are soft and the liquid is reduced by half. You have to stay with this sauce. Strain the liquid, pressing well. Have ready a saucepan of boiling water.

Beat up the egg yolks in a basin and place over the boiling water, stir in the vinegar and keep stirring, then gradually add the butter, a small dob at a time, strengthening the whisking action with each addition. Add plenty of ground black pepper and a touch of salt and whisk again. The sauce should be thick with a good tangy flavor. As a salad and sauce ingredient, as a garnish, chopped and mixed into cream and cottage cheese, added to soups, casseroles, rice, meat and chicken dishes, A. *fistulosum* has few equals. The color of the leaves gives interest, the taste enlivens the dish and food value is increased.

MEDICINAL USE: Antiseptic, diuretic, expectorant.

The shallot-type onion shares the attributes of its relation the onion proper and can be expected to aid the human body in the same way although more gently.

SHEPHERD'S PURSE — Mother's Heart, Pickpurse, St James's Wort

Botanical name: *Capsella bursa-pastoris*
Family: *Cruciferae*
Part used: Whole Plant

Shepherd's purse is a persistent weed in temperate zones of the world. A little annual plant, it crops up on unproductive stony ground, on riverbanks and anywhere it can get the right sort of foothold. It looks insignificant; the leaves are narrow and toothed and the cluster of small white flowers at the top of the stem are followed by little seedpods, heart-shaped or triangular, presumably like the shape of the purse shepherds used to carry in the old days.

The plant is a prodigious seed-producer—how many other plants can ripen almost half a million seeds in a season?

MEDICINAL USE: Stimulant, diuretic, styptic.

A tea made from the dried plant, taken in wineglassful doses, will arrest internal bleeding, ease cystitis and act on stones in the bladder and kidneys and also control diarrhea.

A heavy nosebleed will soon stop if the nostril is plugged with cotton-wool soaked in a decoction of the plant. In desperate cases, the leaves, etc., can be pounded to extract the juice rapidly. The plant is also said to be good for arteriosclerosis. Shepherd's purse is prescribed in homoeopathic dosage for excessive menses and as a womb tonic. An old recipe says that the chopped-up herb, left to steep in wine for a week and then strained, will, when taken in tablespoonful doses on the hour, quickly relieve heavy menstrual pain. The plant is seldom used medicinally today but it still has its active constituents, which include choline, amino-phenol, diosmin and acetylchlorine and tyramine. If you find any in your garden and decide to dry it for use, don't bother to keep it for more than a season as its properties are soon lost.

SLIPPERY ELM — Red Elm, Moose Elm
Botanical name: *Ulmus rubra or fulva*
Family: *Ulmaceae*
Part used: Inner bark

This tall deciduous tree is a native of Central and North America. The toothed leaves are a dark green and the tiny red flowers just tufts of stamens growing from the calyx. The outer bark is rough; it is the inner bark of the tree that gives slippery elm such importance. Bought from an herbalist it comes in long folded strips, pinky-brown in color and with a faintly yeasty scent; it is quite tough and fibrous but the meal it contains is obvious when it is split.

CULINARY USE
The powdered bark, mixed with water or milk and sweetened with the optional addition of a little spice, makes a surprisingly palatable invalid food which can be easily digested when little

else is tolerated. It has quite as much food value as oatmeal. It makes a very good food for babies who are having trouble with their digestion.

MEDICINAL USE: Emollient, diuretic, pectoral.

The mucilage in the bark makes it a good emollient for an inflamed digestive or eliminative tract and throat and bronchial tubes. The bark itself can be used soaked in water but it is probably easier to use it powdered and mixed with water. Inflammation in any part of the body will be eased by the intake of slippery elm bark—it is a great soother. An enema of 1 ounce (30g) powdered bark to 2½ cups (600mL) boiling water will, when cool enough to use, bring relief to inflamed bowels. Mixed with hot water and made into a sticky paste, it will draw out the poison from septic wounds and ulcers—messy if used directly on the skin and just as effective if spread on muslin before application.

Beaten into Vaseline, it can make a good ointment and an even better one if boiled up with equal quantities of white lard and beeswax. If you ask around, you may find some proprietary brands available. The ointment is good to have on hand for the "bad knees" of children, chilblains, burns and cuts; it cleanses, soothes and speeds healing.

SOAPWORT — Bouncing Bet, Fuller's Herb
Botanical name: *Saponaria officinalis*
Family: *Caryophyllaceae*
Parts used: Leaves, roots and stems

Soapwort grows wild in many temperate areas of the western hemisphere and can make a pretty, though not conspicuous, garden plant. It grows to about 3 feet (1m) high, but the stems are weak and it sprawls rather badly. The pale green leaves are smooth and pointed, the pale pink flowers (often double in the cultivated variety) have a long thin calyx and little scent although both leaves and root have a strong one—a bit on the bitter, musty side.

Although so useful medicinally, it does not seem to have spread to other temperate parts of the world. But if you are fortunate to come across it, give it good soil, some shade and plenty of moisture. It can be raised fairly easily from seed and then propagated by dividing up the rootstock.

MEDICINAL USE: Alterative, detergent.

The root is the part most commonly used; dosage is small. One ounce (30g) root boiled up in 1¼ cups (300mL) water should be taken in tablespoonful doses no more than 3 times a day for jaundice, gout and obstinate pimples. It should always be taken when freshly prepared. It is also said to be good for angina.

It is probably best taken in homoeopathic preparation. Saponaria (so called because of the saponin content of the plant) is excellent for skin complaints.

HOUSEHOLD USE

The leaves or root, boiled up and then gently simmered, produce a soapy liquid that not only makes a good shampoo but is good for washing wool and any other delicate material.

SOLOMON'S SEAL — Ladies' Lockets

Botanical name: *Polygonatum multiflora*
Family: *Liliaceae*
Part used: Root

This curiously named plant grows wild in parts of northern Europe and can be cultivated in other areas where the winter is not too cold and the summer not too hot. The round, smooth stems which grow at least 20 inches (50cm) high curve and then droop downwards; the dark-green pointed leaves grow alternately along the stem with creamy-white bell-shaped flowers growing on short stalks from the leaf axils.

The flowers are followed by small black berries. The waxy, yellowish root is a knobbly rhizome and presumably the plant got its name from the way the root is marked by oval scars left by the stems. The plant can be grown from seed or increased by chopping the rhizome into sections that carry roots and replanting each piece. The plant grows best in shade where there is plenty of leaf mold.

MEDICINAL USE: Astringent, demulcent, tonic.

The general opinion today is that the root should not be used as an internal medication, but at one time it was well used in conjunction with other herbs in cases of tuberculosis where there was bleeding from the lungs.

It is still used however, powdered or fresh, to make a poultice for wounds that are slow to heal, bruises and inflamed piles. The old herbalist Gerard thought it was an herb that should be grown in every garden; he recommended it strongly to willful women who brought on themselves the domestic black eye.

SORREL

Botanical name: *Rumex acetosa*
Species: *R. scutatus*
Family: Polygonaceae
Parts used: Leaves and flowers

The common sorrel, *R. acetosa*, is a perennial plant found growing wild throughout Europe and Asia and other temperate parts of the world—*R. scutatus*, the French sorrel, is a cultivated type. The wild plant grows to about 3 feet (1m) high with oblong narrow-pointed leaves and spikes of rusty-red flowers thickly clustered on tiny stems growing from a main stem; the cultivated one is of much lower growth with fleshier leaves which contain much less acid.

French sorrel can be grown from seed and increased by root division. It can be an invasive garden plant, so, although handsome enough, container-growth should be considered. The plants need a good soil, full sun and plenty of moisture.

CULINARY USE

The leaves have a sharp, lemony, rather bitter taste. They can be used in soup, mayonnaise and salads. The young leaves, chopped and cooked in butter, are not unpleasant. Try them with a plain or mushroom omelet or added to white sauce.

SORREL SOUP

Sauté equal quantities sliced potato and sorrel leaves, well-chopped with a little chopped onion in margarine or butter until the potato is soft—10-15 minutes. Stir to prevent too much browning. Add stock (bought cubes can be used) and simmer for 10 minutes.

When cool enough, pour into a blender and blend until smooth. Season with a little salt and plenty of ground black pepper. Alternatively, rub through a fine sieve. Cream can either be added just before serving or a swirl of cream can be patterned over the soup after it has been poured into individual soup bowls.

SORREL MAYONNAISE

Beat together or blend in a food processor 1 egg, 1 tablespoonful lemon juice, 1 tablespoon sorrel leaves very finely chopped, 1 teaspoonful mustard powder and 1 crushed garlic clove, if desired. Then add 1 cup of olive oil, very, very gradually and beat until desired thickness is obtained.

Do not attempt to dry sorrel leaves for use in cooking—use them either fresh or frozen. Wrapped in foil, they keep well in the freezer part of the refrigerator and soon defrost for use.

MEDICINAL USE: Refrigerant, diuretic.

A tea made from the young leaves makes a sharp-tasting cooling drink, which will also cleanse the system and provide some Vitamin C. It is quite useful when bladder, liver or kidneys are not functioning well.

People with a tendency toward rheumatism or renal colic should not use sorrel, neither should asthma sufferers.

HOUSEHOLD USE

The stems and flowers of the wild variety, when dried, can be used in dried flower arrangements.

Since the plant contains oxalic acid, a strong tea will remove stains from silver and have an effect on verdigris on other metals. The juice of fresh leaves will loosen ink stains, which can then be washed out.

SOUTHERNWOOD — Old Man, Lad's Love

Botanical name: *Artemesia abrotanum*
Family: *Compositae*
Part used: Leaves

Southernwood, a native of southern Europe, makes an excellent garden plant in all temperate areas, though it will not flower unless it has sufficient heat. Since the leaves are the most decorative part of the plant, this does not really matter.

It makes a smallish perennial shrub with gray-green narrow leaves that grow in a feathery profusion and have a clean lemony scent. Young plants should be given full sun and some moisture but once they are established they can take a little neglect.

The seeds take so long to germinate that propagation is best done from cuttings and root division. A straggly southernwood looks really unkempt so judicious pruning and shaping are necessary—don't be afraid of a hard cutback if the plant is getting out of hand, but do it early in the year to enable growth to re-establish safely.

MEDICINAL USE: Stimulant, antiseptic, emmenogoguic, tonic, astringent, nervine.

Southernwood tea, made by pouring boiling water over the leaves, has a bitter taste and needs sweetening to make it palatable—a good pinch of dried leaves to a cup of boiling water is quite enough for most people. This tea has a pronounced effect on female reproductive organs and will promote the menstrual flow and have a good toning effect. The leaves contain the essential oil absinthol, once widely used in the making of absinth but, due to worry over the deleterious effect it can produce if used over long periods, now superseded by the use of aniseed, but, in short-term use, southernwood used with water makes an excellent tonic which stimulates the appetite and acts as a restorative after debilitating illness.

The powdered leaves mixed with treacle or honey, and taken in teaspoonful doses, will help the body to expel threadworms.

COSMETIC USE

The herb is supposed to be useful against baldness although information as to exactly how it is used is hard to come by. In the old days it seems that the herb was burned and the ashes were mixed with oil and then applied to the scalp—or even to the chin to promote beard growth, which is no doubt why the plant was called lad's love. Since these appellations are not given without reason, investigation could prove fruitful.

HOUSEHOLD USE

Moths, ants and other insects do not like the scene of southernwood, so sachets in wardrobes and under carpets make a good repellent.

IN THE GARDEN

The fruit fly and the mosquito do not like the scent either so it is a good plant to position near garden ponds and fruit trees. Chickens will be freer from lice if southernwood is grown in the run. We all know what a wasteland they can make of an enclosure and what an eyesore it can be; they don't seem to want to scratch up southernwood, so plant it for your own benefit as well as theirs.

SUNFLOWER

Botanical name: *Helianthus annuus*
Family: *Compositae annuus*
Part used: Seeds

Sunflowers are among the tallest flowering plants with strong erect stems, large lightly-toothed and strongly veined leaves and huge yellow daisy-shaped flowers—many-petalled and stamened. They are grown commercially for the seed in climates which resemble that of Central America, their native home.

They also make handsome garden plants in more temperate parts of the world. If you decide to grow them, be prepared to give them lots of water, rich soil and full sun. Bees love them because they produce so much nectar.

CULINARY USE

The seeds are a rich food source, but they need to be husked. They provide protein, calcium and Vitamins E and B. They are good eaten raw but even tastier if given a light coating of oil and roasted carefully until golden-brown.

A healthy drink can be made by blending a half-cup sunflower seeds with 2 tablespoonfuls honey in 2-3 cups water and a good toffee by adding a cup of seeds to a "toffee mixture" made by boiling up a cup of sugar and 3 ounces (90g) butter in a half-cup of water and holding at the boil without stirring until it turns golden-brown.

As soon as you have stirred the seeds into the mixture, spread it out in an oiled tin and mark into sections while still warm. Snap into pieces when cold and store in a closed tin. The oil extracted from the seed is sold commercially and has high nutritive value.

SWEET CICELY — Shepherd's Needle

Botanical name: *Myrrhis odorata*
Family: *Umbelliferae*
Parts used: Leaves, seeds and roots

This tall perennial can reach 5 feet (1.5m) in height and where it grows in the wild can be confused with cow parsley; the leaves, however, have their own scent, somewhere between aniseed and licorice. It also makes a good garden plant.

The leaves resemble those of parsley but are lightly hairy on the underside and the stems too carry fine hairs. The white umbelliferous flowers produce long seed-heads, which darken as they ripen and take root quickly wherever they fall. Since the leaves are the most valuable part of the plant, flowering and seeding should be restricted to use. Sweet cicely is an undemanding plant as to soil but needs space and some shade.

CULINARY USE

The leaves have a sugar content tolerated by diabetics so are useful in the sweetening of tart fruits, etc. The green seeds give flavor to salads; the ripe ones to fruit pies. They have a stronger flavor.

The roots can be used raw in salads or boiled as a vegetable and even candied. They are quite good stir-fried too. Try a sweet cicely tea—but made from the fresh leaves; this herb does not dry particularly well but, fortunately, has a long season in the garden.

MEDICINAL USE

Tea made from the leaves makes a mild and pleasant tonic.

HOUSEHOLD USE

The crushed seeds were once very popular as a furniture polish. If you pound the seeds and strain off the oil it can be added to bought wax polish to give additional oil and fragrance.

TANSY — Bachelor's Buttons

Botanical name: *Tanecetum vulgare* **or** *Chrysanthemum vulgare*
Family: *Compositae*
Parts used: Flowers, leaves and roots

Tansy is a decorative perennial plant that grows to about 3 feet (1m) in height and has dark green finely divided feathery leaves and small yellow button-shaped flowers that grow in umbels; it has a camphorish scent. A native of northern Europe, it has become quite widely cultivated in other parts of the world as a decorative garden plant. Accustomed to waste places in the wild, it is tolerant of less-than-perfect garden conditions and will seed freely.

The rhizome root is strong and quick-spreading and can be easily divided. Once a popular medicinal plant, it is now seldom used as modern knowledge has decreed that the oil contained in the leaves could be toxic, particularly when used by pregnant women.

CULINARY USE

The leaves have a ginger-like taste and can be used as a flavoring for savory dishes, soups and stews.

MEDICINAL USE: Soothing, insecticide, disinfectant.

A poultice made from the bruised leaves will ease the pain of sprains and bruises.

COSMETIC USE

Tansy tea made from the leaves makes a good face-wash for acne sufferers. It has an "exfoliant" ability by reason of the hormone it contains and can peel off dead layers of skin and so give a fresher cleaner look to the complexion. Use in small quantity to begin with—some people react more strongly than others.

HOUSEHOLD USE

Tansy hung in the kitchen and larder will keep away flies. In the wardrobe it will keep away silverfish, fleas and moths. Liberally strewn in kennels and pet baskets, it will keep pets free from fleas. Rub it well into their coats too, to make the best of the tanecitin oil it contains.

IN THE GARDEN

Grown under fruit trees, it will repel pests. Rub the leaves between your fingers as you pass to release the scent.

Never burn discarded tansy plants—add them to the compost for they contain not only the useful oil but potassium and other minerals.

TARRAGON

Botanical name: *Artemesia dranunculus*
Family: *Compositae*
Part used: Leaves

Tarragon, a close relative of southernwood and wormwood, is a warm-weather plant that demands the right conditions before it will consent to do well. It needs a light dryish soil with plenty of sunshine for part of the day, and shade for the rest of it in summer, and protection in winter against both wind and rain.

If the soil gets too wet the roots will rot. The seeds are mostly infertile so, if you have a plant, increase it by root division and do it gently. Don't chop the root, pull it apart and replant any sections that show signs of putting up a shoot. The leaves are narrow and long, a tender pale green when young, darkening with age. If any flowers should show, nip them out. They are quite unremarkable anyway.

There are two varieties of tarragon, the French and the Russian. If buying the plant from a nursery, make certain to get the French one. The Russian one is larger, but the leaves have little flavor. Both types are decorative. Tarragon leaves lose their valuable volatile oil when dried, so a plant in the garden should be the aim as, apart from its well-known culinary virtues, it has medicinal ones too.

CULINARY USE

The sharp clean taste of the leaves makes them good to use in sauces, mayonnaise, vinegar, chicken, fish and egg dishes, not to mention veal and rabbit. One of the simplest and nicest ways to use them is to chop them very finely with an equal amount of chopped chives and to beat them into cottage or cream cheese with a dash of lemon juice and then use as a sandwich filling. They can also be used sprinkled over soup, meat and vegetables.

The things to remember about tarragon are that long cooking makes it taste nasty, and that you should never use much. A few leaves go a long way.

If you add it to a white sauce, add it near the end of cooking time. This goes for tarragon, hollandaise and bearnaise sauce. A clear soup made from chicken or fish stock will earn plaudits if chopped tarragon is added during the final boil-up. Tarragon vinegar is made by pouring wine vinegar over a jar of well-packed fresh tarragon leaves and leaving it to steep in a warm place for 2-3 weeks. Use strained. An inferior vinegar is possible by steeping a good 1 ounce (30g) bought dried tarragon to 2½ cups (600mL) wine vinegar and leaving for a fortnight before using. I find even this better than the bought tarragon vinegar, though I don't like the bits. Some people feel they give an "herby" look, however.

MEDICINAL USE: Stomachic, aperitif.

Tarragon tea made with 1 ounce (30g) leaves to 4 cups (1L) of boiling water is good for a stomach blown up with wind. It is also said to ease the pain of rheumatism and to give appetite.

THISTLE — Blessed Thistle

Botanical name: *Carduus benedictus*
Family: *Compositae*
Parts used: Leaves and flowers

There has to be something very special about a thistly plant that earns
the name "blessed." It got its name in the time of Bede and was well known
to the Romans who made certain to bring it Britain with them on their
great conquering forays. A native of the wastelands of southern Europe, it
is an annual plant of medium height with prickly white-veined leaves and
large, drooping, purple flowers. It grows well from seed in any temperate
climate and is not fussy about soil; it looks good in the garden.

CULINARY USE

The roots can be eaten, boiled, and the flowers too, peeling them as one would a globe
artichoke. This information is probably useless as the plant is seldom grown in enough quantity
to warrant it.

MEDICINAL USE: Tonic, diaphoretic and for female complaints.

You may find the dried leaves supplied by an herbalist. They can be used to make an infusion
to act either as a tonic, drunk cold, or as an inducement to bring on perspiration during feverish
complaints, drunk hot. An overdose can empty the bowels at great speed. Beyond these facts
information about the blessed thistle is hard to come by in detail; there are many references
in old herbals as to its efficacy in strengthening both heart, lungs and the lactation ability of
mothers and for its ability to correct hormone imbalance. This last information was implied
rather than spelled out but must be worth checking. Lists of the complaints it can help range
from arthritis to vaginal discharge. Somewhere, sometime, somebody found it useful in every one
of them or the knowledge would not have been passed on and the thistle would never have been
called "blessed."

THYME

Botanical name: *Thymus*
Family: *Labiatae*
Part used: Leaves

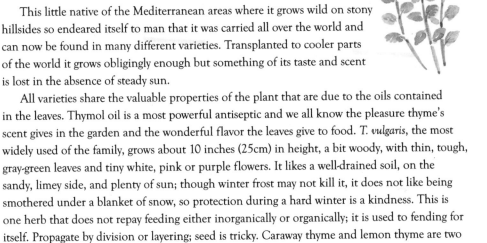

This little native of the Mediterranean areas where it grows wild on stony hillsides so endeared itself to man that it was carried all over the world and can now be found in many different varieties. Transplanted to cooler parts of the world it grows obligingly enough but something of its taste and scent is lost in the absence of steady sun.

All varieties share the valuable properties of the plant that are due to the oils contained in the leaves. Thymol oil is a most powerful antiseptic and we all know the pleasure thyme's scent gives in the garden and the wonderful flavor the leaves give to food. *T. vulgaris*, the most widely used of the family, grows about 10 inches (25cm) in height, a bit woody, with thin, tough, gray-green leaves and tiny white, pink or purple flowers. It likes a well-drained soil, on the sandy, limey side, and plenty of sun; though winter frost may not kill it, it does not like being smothered under a blanket of snow, so protection during a hard winter is a kindness. This is one herb that does not repay feeding either inorganically or organically; it is used to fending for itself. Propagate by division or layering; seed is tricky. Caraway thyme and lemon thyme are two of the popular culinary varieties and there are smaller-leaved creeping ones which are lovely for the rockery, for edgings, or between stones on a path. *T. serphyllum* can be used to make a small lawn where traffic is not too heavy.

CULINARY USE

The leaves can be used fresh, either alone or in a *bouquet garni*, in meat, chicken, rabbit and vegetable stews and soups, in stuffings, sauces, pickles, vinegars, etc. They go particularly well with onions, mushrooms, beetroot and zucchini. A few bruised leaves rubbed over a piece of meat which is to be kept in the refrigerator for a day or two before use will both preserve it and give it better flavor. Thyme is so widely used in cooking it is hardly necessary to list its uses.

MEDICINAL USE: Tonic, antiseptic, antispasmodic, deodorant, parasitic.

Thyme tea is good for all chest ailments—Culpeper recommended it for children with "chin-cough." It tastes very nice flavored with honey.

It makes a good tonic, particularly after flu or for slight anemia and can be used as a gargle for a sore throat or as a protection when germs are about. Taken after a heavy fatty meal, it will relieve wind and take away the feeling of nausea. Thyme tea drunk as soon as the first evidence of migraine shows is said to shorten the duration of the attack. The best antidote to migraine, however, is swift dosage with the biochemic tissue salt, natrum sulphate.

The leaves, boiled up in a covered saucepan to retain the antiseptic oils, give a liquid which, when strained, makes an excellent lotion for bathing cuts and wounds.

COSMETIC USE

Oil of thyme is good in the bath, so is a strong thyme tea, strained. The tea makes a good rinse for the hair. If the hair is falling, spend time rubbing the tea into the scalp. If there is any real worry, boil up the leaves and keep at the boil until the liquid is reduced by half and, when cool, use that.

IN THE GARDEN

Some thyme growing near cabbages will keep away cabbage-root fly; failing that try sprinkling some dried sage around the plants.

TURMERIC
Botanical name: Circuma longa
Family: Ziniberaceae
Part used: Root

Turmeric is a native of southern Asia and is cultivated in other tropical parts of the world. It is a strong-growing perennial plant with long narrow leaves and spikes of 5-petalled yellow flowers. The fruits are capsuled. The root, for which the plant is grown, is a rhizome that contains a water-soluble yellow pigment and an essential oil.

CULINARY USE

The root can be bought at herbalists or delicatessens, either in pieces or powdered. It has a very light sharpish taste and scent, not unlike that of its relative, ginger. It is mainly used as an ingredient of curry powder or as a food colorant. It is much less expensive than saffron and gives the same good rich color. The familiar mustard pickle owes its color to the addition of turmeric to the recipe. The flavor is too light to be depended on by itself, turmeric is mostly used for eye-appeal.

MEDICINAL USE: Carminative.

Although used in India as an aid to digestion, turmeric is practically never used medicinally in the Western world.

HOUSEHOLD USE

The root can make a yellow dye and is much used for that purpose in the East, but unless alum is used to fix it, it easily washes out. I have been unable to find precise instructions as to how to use it.

UVA-URSI — Bearberry

Botanical name: *Arctostaphylos uva-ursi*
Family: *Ericaceae*
Part used: Leaves

An evergreen shrub with pointed, oval, shiny leaves, uva-ursi has been used as a medicinal herb in northern Europe since the Middle Ages. The dried leaves are still sold by herbalists all over the world.

MEDICINAL USE: Astringent, diuretic, female complaints.

A tea can be used for digestive troubles but should be used only as long as disturbance persists because of its high tannin content. Its main use is as a disinfectant for the urinary tract and as a vaginal douche in cases of leucorrhoea. It can help in bed-wetting and is good as a temporary help for a disturbed spleen.

VALERIAN

Botanical name: *Valeriana officinalis*
Family: *Valerianaceae*
Part used: Roots

Valerian has a long tradition as a medicinal plant and many of the more decorative varieties find their way into gardens but if you wish to grow it for use as a medicine be sure to get *V. officinalis* for this is the only one of any value.

It makes quite a tall plant with finely divided leaves and small clusters of little pink flowers, which grow from small leaf-axils at the top of the stem. It likes full sun and is not particular as to soil. Propagation can be made by division of the rhizome, which is short and quite thick.

The roots take two seasons to become of use and should be dried slowly in a dark, dry place. Fortunately this means they must be kept away from other herbs set to dry. Both cats and rats love its smell and could be attracted to it so a wire-mesh as a cover could be useful.

MEDICINAL USE: Anodyne, antispasmodic, nervine.

Valerian provides an excellent sedative with absolutely no side effects, so it could be worthwhile trying to acquire the taste. One ounce (30g) root to 2½ cups (600mL) boiling water taken in wineglassful doses when cool is one way of taking it. An addition of honey helps. You could also leave a small piece of root to steep in a little water overnight.

You can buy it both in powdered form and as a tincture. The powder can be taken with jam or honey and the drops of tincture in honey and water. This stress on ameliorating the taste may be unnecessary as I am told many people soon adjust to it, particularly when they find how much good the medicine does.

It was once regarded as the main hope for epileptics and is certainly good for hysteria and spasms, giddiness and migraine, breathlessness and palpitations. It will ease the headaches and miseries associated with the menopause, make sleep come more easily and prevent gas forming in the stomach. It is also said to be good for gravel in the bladder. On the whole, valerian tea is best made by the use of cold water—the root should never be boiled. Dosage should not be too frequent and too strong a preparation could be counterproductive and bring on headache and restlessness. The water in which some root has been macerating makes a soothing wash for sore or rubbed skin.

VANILLA

Botanical name: *Vanilla planifolia*
Family: *Orchidaceae*
Part used: Bean pods

Vanilla, native to the West Indies, Java, Mexico and Madagascar, is a handsome climbing orchid with large fleshy leaves and yellow, fleshy flowers, rather dull in color, which are succeeded by large, fleshy seedpods. Unlike most spices, the plant does not produce an oil and the seedpods have to be fermented in order to induce them to produce crystals which have the flavor so well known to so many generations of cooks.

CULINARY USE

The pods can be bought whole or ground and are used to give flavor to cakes, puddings, ice-cream and any dish that contains chocolate.

When buying the pods, examine them to make sure they are not split and that there are plenty of crystals. You can cut them into short lengths, use them in cooking, remove them, dry them, store them and use them again and again. Only a short length is needed. Vanilla sugar is made just by storing a piece of pod in the sugar container. Vanilla essence is obtainable commercially but beware the synthetic essence, which is not made from vanilla at all. The best use for this is for washing down the shelves of the refrigerator. A few drops of the real essence will flavor icings, egg custards, fruit salads, etc.

VERBENA

Botanical name: *Lippia citriodora*
Family: *Verbenaceae*
Part used: Leaves

Lemon verbena, as it is commonly called because of the delicious lemony taste of its leaves, is a small deciduous shrub with pale green pointed leaves and even paler lavender-colored flowers, which grow in panicles at the end of the stems. It needs warmth and shelter and a trim every now and again to prevent straggling. Some people in colder areas bring the plant indoors during a bout of bad weather. If you do, go easy on watering as it could rot. It can be propagated from heeled cuttings.

CULINARY USE

The chopped leaves give a lemon flavoring to salads, fish dishes, fruit drinks, jams and jellies, etc. Use as for lemon rind.

MEDICINAL USE: Digestive, sedative.

Tea made from the leaves is a gentle sedative and will help to clear mucus from the bronchial tubes and sinuses. Taken after a heavy meal it will aid digestion.

COSMETIC USE

Lemon verbena is used in the manufacture of scents and colognes.

HOUSEHOLD USE

The dried leaves make a useful inclusion to potpourris and scented sachets as they hold their scent so well.

VERVAIN

Botanical name: *Verbena officinalis*
Family: *Verbenaceae*
Part used: Herb

This is the medicinal member of the verbena family—the lemon-scented verbena not only looks quite different but has different properties. Vervain grows wild by the side of the road and on dry chalky grassland, an unremarkable-looking, medium-sized plant with rough leaves heavily notched around the edges and spikes of pale mauve flowers. The ancients called it the "magic herb"—it was even regarded as sacred by the Druids.

Well into the 18th century, country people hung sprigs of it outside their doorways to prevent the entry of evil spirits or used it as a personal talisman hung around the neck. It was the chief ingredient of the love-philtre, which desperate and abandoned lovers used to regain former happiness. If the local witch was thought to have cast a spell, vervain could be depended on to lift it. It is certainly a powerful herb; modern analysis has established that it contains two glycosides, tannin, a bitter compound and essential oil and it is still held in respect.

MEDICINAL USE: Nervine, tonic, expectorant, emetic, sudorific, emmenogoguic, vermifuge.

Vervain tea made from the leaves and flowering tops, taken in wineglassful doses, is good for headaches, colds and fevers (a larger dose taken before bedtime will often "break" a cold by morning). Regular dosage will aid sufferers from bronchitis, asthma and the "shakes." It will bring on delayed menstruation or increase scanty menstrual flow. Women who suffer discomfort and headaches during what has become a monthly tribulation should certainly try vervain tea. Dried leaves can be bought. The tea can also be used to wash wounds and ulcers to help them to heal; cotton-wool pads soaked in it and pressed to the temples will relieve headache and neuralgia. Gargle with the tea if your gums are unhealthy and your breath bad. If lumbago has you bent double, make a fat poultice of vervain, either fresh or dried, and use that, as hot as possible. Some say it is better to make the poultice from leaves that have been soaked and then boiled up in a little vinegar. Vervain tea will help the body to expel worms. This herb has such a pronounced effect on both the liver and the nerves that it has to be regarded as a first line of defense. If you feel sickly, short on energy, tearful, shivery or bloated, and if you have that "yellow" look, make a pot of vervain tea.

VIOLET — Sweet Violet
Botanical name: *Viola odorata*
Family: *Violaceae*
Parts used: Leaves and flowers

The violet is known in temperate areas all over the world; a much-loved plant that not only grows in the wild but adapts readily to cultivation. It has sweet-smelling flowers and heart-shaped leaves. In the wild it has single flowers of a shade which has given its name to a color and an unmistakable fragrance; in cultivation the flowers can be either single or double and of a color ranging from deep purple through pink to white and yellow—fragrance is variable. There are hundreds of varieties of violet obtainable.

In Australia, the tiny creeping plant, which is such a good groundcover, can make a sudden welcome appearance in a garden—*Viola hederacea* is the wild violet of the southern hemisphere.

The medicinal properties of the violet have been celebrated since the earliest days when plants came under scrutiny for their possible usefulness to man; the Greeks and Romans found both culinary and cosmetic use for it too.

Violet wine—how did they make it? No recipe seems to have survived and much else has been forgotten too. This plant, the symbol of modesty, has little to be modest about, for it is not only beautiful but wonderfully useful.

Once you have introduced violets into the garden they can always be there for the plant spreads by sending out creeping runners. Cut off a section of the runner which carries healthy roots and replant and stock will soon be increased. *Viola hederaceae* needs watching though it seems to resent interference. Violets like good soil and partial shade.

CULINARY USE

Toss a few flowers into a salad to give it color; they are edible. The flowers can be candied for decoration for cakes, trifles, etc. Dip fresh flowers in well-beaten white of egg, lightly roll them in fine sugar and leave to dry on grease-proof paper. When candied, the flowers should be kept in an airproof tin against the day when panic measures are indicated.

Plain vanilla ice-cream served in a tall glass with a decoration of candied violets can save a desperate hostess.

MEDICINAL USE: Antiseptic, expectorant.

The infusion made from flowers and leaves has a gentle laxative effect and will help the coughing up of phlegm and even ease the symptoms of "bad nerves."

Violet syrup, made by boiling up a good handful of leaves and flowers in sugar and water, makes a dosage acceptable to children suffering from whooping cough. The most spectacular claim made for the violet is that the leaves can be useful in the treatment of cancer; a tea taken internally and used as an external fomentation of the warm liquor is recommended. Such measures can do no harm, the good can only be known if the method is used.

Country people have long known that a warm poultice of fresh bruised violet leaves will ease the pain of the cracked nipples of nursing mothers. A cool decoction of the violet, soaked in cotton wool and pressed against the forehead and temples, was once a sovereign remedy for the headaches of those who had looked too well upon the wine. It worked then, so why not now?

WITCH-HAZEL — Spotted Alder, Winterbloom, Snapping Hazelnut

Botanical name: *Hamamelis virginiana*
Family: *Hamamelidaceae*
Parts used: Bark and leaves

Witch-hazel is a North American native, a small tree that will consent to grow elsewhere where the climate is right but is often reluctant to produce its seed. The shrub rarely makes more than 13 feet (4m) in height, has a smooth, grayish bark, leaves that are readily recognized as resembling those of the European hazel and stringy yellow flowers that make an appearance independently of the leaves.

The shrub requires a coolish climate, rich soil and plenty of moisture. It is not the most decorative plant in the world and since the extract, distilled from leaves and bark, can be readily bought, not a plant a gardener need feel he must prove able to grow.

MEDICINAL USE: Astringent, tonic, sedative.

A decoction made from the bark or leaves can be used as an enema to help bleeding piles. The liquid from the boiling up of leaves and bark, added to Vaseline and beaten in, will make a soothing ointment for the same complaint and will shrink the piles. It is possible to buy suppositories that contain witch hazel. Dried witch-hazel can be bought and used, in infusion, as a nasal and vaginal douche, particularly where the local veins give throbbing pain; witch-hazel is a marvelous decongestive and aids the circulation of the blood. Wounds slow to heal will be helped by witch-hazel's astringent properties.

COSMETIC USE

Witch-hazel, bought from a pharmacist, is widely used to tighten open pores and give the facial skin a smoother appearance; it can be dabbed neat on spots or used with rosewater (3 parts rosewater to one of witch-hazel) to dry up an oily skin. Any astringent herb should be used with care—witch-hazel is no exception.

WOOD BETONY — Bishopswort

Botanical name: *Stachys officinalis*
Family: *Labiatae*
Part used: Herb

Wood betony is found growing wild in shady woods in Europe and Britain and in some other temperate parts of the world. A member of the nettle family, it has a hairy, tall stem with large leaves, round-toothed and dark green, which decrease in size up the stem. The flowers are reddish-purple with white splotches and grow in spikes. The root is a creeping rhizome.

The root, which has a very nasty taste, has understandably never been used medicinally as it causes heavy vomiting. The fresh leaves are not recommended either—they should be bought dried.

MEDICINAL USE: Alterative, astringent, tonic.

Wood betony is mostly used today in conjunction with other herbs as a digestive or sedative. The Romans used it when epidemics were around or when they felt threatened by witchcraft. The astringent oil contained in the fresh leaves can, to some extent, be released from the dried ones by gently boiling them up in a covered saucepan. The strained liquid can then be used to dress cuts and stings which are beginning to go "bad."

WOODRUFF — Waldmeister Tea

Botanical name: *Asperula odorata*
Family: *Rubiaceae*
Part used: Whole plant

Woodruff is a small plant, no more than 8 inches (20cm) high, which likes shade and a soil rich in leaf mold. It grows in temperate climates, has shiny leaves, dark green with strange little hooks around the edges. It looks rather like goosegrass.

The tiny white flowers, surprisingly sweet-scented, are star-shaped and grow in rather floppy whorls at the top of the stems. A wild plant in many temperate parts of the world, it consents to cultivation. Propagate by root division.

The attraction of woodruff is its scent, which is clean and sweet. To get the best of it the whole plant should be cut when the flowers are at their best and slowly dried before powdering for use in potpourris and scented sachets.

MEDICINAL USE: Tonic, diuretic.

Woodruff tea made from the chopped herb tastes quite pleasant and acts as a general tonic. It clears the liver and is good for the stomach.

THE COMPLETE BOOK OF HERBS & SPICES

WORMWOOD – Old Woman

Botanical name: *Artemesia absinthium*
Family: *Compositae*
Part used: Herb

There are many varieties of this bushy perennial and it grows in many parts
of the world. It is a good-looking plant with a stem which can reach nearly
3 feet (1m) in height with deeply divided silver-gray leaves, slightly fuzzy and
greeny-yellow flowers that grow on short stalks from the leaf-axils.

Common wormwood grows wild on waste ground; the cultivated types will
tolerate both sun and part-shade and, because the roots are strong and penetrate deep into the
soil, can withstand drought. This is a good plant to grow on a clayey soil. Propagation can be
made from cuttings and by division of the plant.

Tall plants can sometimes need support but judicious trimming and removal of the older
parts will keep them sturdy. Beach wormwood (*A. stellerana*) is lower-growing and spreads
rapidly; its leaves are paler than those of the common wormwood and feel like a silky felt.
Fringed wormwood or mountain fringe (*A. frigida*) is lower-growing still and makes a lovely
ground cover.

Roman wormwood (*A. pontica*) makes a small, heavily branched shrub. All the wormwoods
are decorative and are much used in "gray" gardens.

CULINARY USE

The taste is too bitter to be used in cooking and its use in the making of the drink absinth
has largely been superseded by the use of less bitter herbs.

MEDICINAL USE: Tonic, stomachic, febrifuge, anthelmintic, disinfectant.

An infusion of 1 ounce (30g) leaves to 2½ cups (600mL) boiling water can be taken in
wineglassful doses to stimulate the appetite—the taste is very bitter. Wormwood has the ability
to stimulate bodily functions and has a beneficial effect on the liver and the reproductive female
organs; it is also good for those who are overweight as it speeds the elimination of food and rids
the system of excess water. The tea is good for expelling worms. The chopped flowers and leaves

can be used as a poultice for bruises and sprains and if left in boiling water for a few minutes, make an emergency disinfectant for cuts and wounds. Moths, fleas and mosquitoes dislike it, so a few sprigs of wormwood can be useful around the house. After you wash the dog, drench the coat with strong wormwood tea; this will get rid of existing fleas and discourage new ones.

IN THE GARDEN

Wormwood roots give off a toxic exudation detrimental to plants growing nearby, even other aromatic plants such as sage and fennel cannot cope with it, but it is a useful plant to grow near fruit trees to guard them against caterpillars, aphids and moths. If slugs are making a regular run, pour the tea over the ground. Mice don't like it either.

YARROW — Soldiers' Woundwort, Military Herb, Thousand Leaf, Nosebleed, Sneezewort, Knight's Milfoil
Botanical name: *Achillea millefolium*
Family: *Compositae*
Part used: Herb

The country names demonstrate the uses of this famous herb that has been a favorite since time immemorial. Its botanical name was given because it was widely held that Achilles depended on it to stop his wounded soldiers from bleeding to death and because the leaves are so finely divided there seem to be thousands of them.

The plant, which can grow to about one ounce (30cm) high, has strong angular stems growing from a creeping rhizome root, dark-green ferny leaves and dense umbels of tiny daisy-like flowers, white or pinky-white. It is found growing in the wild in dry sunny meadows and even on mountain slopes. It needs sun and warmth to enable the leaves to produce its valuable volatile oil.

Cultivated varieties are available. A. filipendulina has yellow flowers, A. millefoliumsammetriese, pink ones. A. argentea—silver yarrow—is a much lower-growing plant with silver leaves and white flowers. A. tomentosa—woolly yarrow—is even lower-growing, and with its dark-green fuzzy leaves and clean yellow flowers makes a pretty ground cover. Yarrow is an excellent plant to have growing in the garden as it gives strength to its neighbors.

CULINARY USE

The young leaves can be chopped and used in a salad.

MEDICINAL USE: Tonic, carminative, diaphoretic, astringent, sternutatory.

Tea made from the leaves and flowers is pleasantly bitter and is excellent for when one is feeling "run-down" and when recovery from flu is taking too long. In cases of chill and heavy cold, a hot drink of the tea at bedtime will open the pores and bring on a cleansing perspiration. Since it has the ability to aid most bodily functions it makes a good first line of defense in digestive upsets, sluggish liver and kidney troubles; it can also help to promote the menstrual flow, regulate the bowels and cleanse the blood. The fresh bruised leaves can be used to make a poultice for wounds and sores such as varicose ulcers and a decoction (2 ounces/60g plant to 4 cups/1L of water, boiled up and held at the boil briefly and then allowed to cool) a good cleansing and healing lotion. The powdered leaves were once used as a snuff to bring on a nosebleed to relieve a persistent headache which demonstrates the homoeopathic principle that what causes can cure. The concentration of the snuff brings on bleeding, the application of a few leaves will staunch it. In homoeopathic doses, yarrow is often prescribed for bleeding, piles, unrelenting nosebleed and an undue loss of blood after a confinement or tooth extraction. Yarrow contains an essential oil which is an antiseptic so a quick first-aid of a few leaves pressed against any cut sustained in the garden is recommended, and chewing some young leaves will give temporary relief from toothache.

COSMETIC USE

Yarrow tea makes a good face wash when the complexion is unduly greasy. Drinking the tea regularly will also help.

IN THE GARDEN

If your soil is deficient in copper you need yarrow as a fertilizer. The tea can be used as a plant medicine. Yarrow added to the compost heap will speed the rotting-down to a remarkable degree.

Part III

Using Herbs and Spices

Medicinal Applications

Herbal medicine may not have the dramatic effect of modern drugs but neither does it have what can be their horrific side effects. Today's cure is never tomorrow's nightmare as thalidomide was. The medicinal properties of herbs have years of sustained proof of efficacy behind them—often many thousands of years—and patience will pay off. Cure or healing may come more slowly than you would like but it will be natural and trouble-free. Conditions which have taken years to build up will take time to correct so in most cases it is as well to settle down to a three-month course of treatment. Drastic illnesses demand emergency treatment—a doctor or a homoeopathic practitioner should be consulted without delay—but for complaints that present no immediate threat of large proportion, the herbal remedy could be the answer. Herbs cleanse the body of toxins as well as doing their job; antibiotics do their jobs but leave toxins in the body. The safest way may be the slowest but is surely worthwhile.

A book of this sort *must not* and *should not* attempt to usurp professional advice. It cannot be too strongly stressed that there is no substitute for the services of the herbalist, doctor or homoeopathic practitioner with long years of study and experience to call on; this is a layman's book with information culled from many sources over a long period of years and all of it has proved useful to somebody at some time.

Some herbs are poisonous—warnings are given. Often a poisonous herb can offer healing when correctly used—where, for instance, would the sufferers from angina be without belladonna? Understanding is important in every sphere of life; taking the trouble to understand how herbs, the green healers, can be used, could be the single most important one acquired.

Medicinal preparation of herbs in the home

The two simplest preparations are those of infusion and decoction.

INFUSION

An infusion is made by pouring boiling water over fresh or dried herbs and allowing it to stand for the properties of the herbs to be released into the water, which can then be drunk as a tea or used as a lotion. As a rule-of-thumb, 1 ounce or 30g dried herb can be taken to equal less than ⅔ ounce (20g) fresh herb.

DECOCTION

A decoction is made by pouring cold water over the fresh or dried herb and boiling for 20 minutes or so until the liquid has reduced by one-third. Barks and roots will require longer boiling than flowers, stems, leaves and seeds.

COMMERCIAL PREPARATIONS

Liquid extracts, tinctures, pills, tablets and capsules are obtainable. Information is freely available from herbalists, health food shops, etc.

ACNE: Burdock, Ladies' Mantle, Nasturtium, Parsley, Soapwort, Tansy.

ALTERATIVE: Burdock, Elder, Golden Seal, Ladies' Bedstraw, Pasque Flower, Poke Root, Red Clover, Sarsaparilla.

ANAEMIA: Alfalfa, Angelica, Ground Ivy, Gentian, Horsetail, Nettle, Thyme. ANTIBIOTIC: Nasturtium.

ANTISEPTIC: Bergamot, Chamomile, Clove, Garlic, Gentian, Horsetail, Juniper, Lavender, Marigold, Melilot, Shallot, Southernwood, Thyme, Yarrow.

APPETITE, Loss of: Angelica, Cardamom, Ginseng, Hops, Mugwort, Quassia, Southernwood, Tarragon, Wormwood.

ARTHRITIS: Aloe, Comfrey, Male Fern (poultice).

ARTERIOSCLEROSIS: Chervil, Couch grass, Garlic, Mistletoe, Shepherd's Purse.

ASTHMA: Coltsfoot, Elecampane Root, Evening Primrose, Golden Seal, Lobelia, Maidenhair Fern, Plantain, Sage, Vervain.

ATHLETE'S FOOT: Red Clover.

BAD BREATH: Caraway, Cinnamon, Vervain. BED WETTING: Nettle seeds, Uva-ursi

BLADDER: Arrowroot (inflammation), Couch grass, Ginseng, Golden Rod, Parsley. Gravel in the bladder: Parsley Piert, Sesame, Shepherd's Purse, Valerian.

BLOOD PURIFIERS: Borage, Dandelion, Gentian, Ginger, Goosegrass, Hops, Nettle, Tansy, Red Clover, Sarsaparilla, Yarrow.

BLOOD PRESSURE
High: Foxglove, Garlic, Ginseng, Mistletoe.
Low: Anise, Balm, Shepherd's Purse.
Regulator: Hawthorn.

BOILS: Burdock, Chamomile, Fenugreek, Flax, Ground Ivy, Nasturtium, Plantain, Sage.

BOWELS: Arrowroot, Slippery Elm (inflammation), Rhubarb (regulator).
Constipation (habitual): Aloe, Cascara Sagrada, Chickweed, Dandelion, Flax, Ginseng, Golden Rod, Senna.

Laxative: Borage, Cowslip, Goosegrass, Horehound, Ladies' Bedstraw, Licorice, Mustard seeds, Nasturtium, Sesame seeds, Violet.

Purgative: Groundsel, Poke Root, Thistle (Blessed).

BRAIN: Chervil, Eyebright.

BRONCHITIS: Coltsfoot, Flax, Garlic, Ginger, Horehound, Horsetail, Lime flowers, Licorice, Maidenhair Fern, Myrtle, Nasturtium, Pansy, Pennyroyal, Sage, Slippery Elm, Thyme, Verbena, Vervain, Violet.

BRUISES and SPRAINS: Arnica, Bay, Comfrey, Hyssop, Marigold, Marjoram, Nettle, St. John's Wort, Solomon's Seal, Tansy, Wormwood.

BURNS and SCALDS: Aloe, Comfrey, Golden Rod, Marigold, Nettle, Plantain, St. John's Wort, Slippery Elm.

CHILBLAINS: Marigold (poultice).

COLDS and CHILLS: Angelica, Balm, Catmint, Chamomile, Cinnamon, Elderflowers, Garlic, Gentian, Ginger, Golden Rod, Licorice, Meadowsweet, Pennyroyal, Raspberry, St. John's Wort, Vervain, Yarrow.

COLITIS: Comfrey, Lobelia, Marshmallow, Slippery Elm.

COUGHS: Anise, Borage, Comfrey, Elecampane, Ground Ivy, Horehound, Hyssop, Licorice, Maidenhair Fern, Marshmallow, Mullein, Savory.

CORNS: Dandelion, Fenugreek, Garlic, Greater Celandine, Marigold.

CRAMP: Catmint (stomach), Cowslip, Pennyroyal. CYSTITIS: Horsetail, Juniper, Lovage, St. John's Wort, Shepherd's Purse.

Culinary Herbs and Spices

The best flavor and best food value are obtained from an herb when it is fresh and green and too many people rely on a few snippets of chives, a stray mint leaf and a scattering of parsley to enliven a plain salad. A brief foray into the garden and some energetic snipping with scissors can provide a desperate hostess, faced with unexpected guests and only a lettuce and some tomatoes to offer, with salvation and a reputation for providing something "different." Anyone with herbs in the garden has flavor on hand.

Lemon balm gives a clean, lemony taste. Burnet and borage taste cucumbery. Basil is clovey and peppery. Mint can taste of apple, orange, pineapple, etc. Tarragon has a sweet anisey flavor. Summer savory is like thyme, only sweeter and milder. Lovage tastes like celery. Nasturtium leaves are peppery. Marjoram is sweet and a bit peppery.

And as edible garnishes, there are the flowers of the nasturtium, rosemary and

DE-TOXICANT: Alfalfa, Red Clover.

DIARRHEA: Cinnamon, Hawthorn, Lime flowers, Meadowsweet, Mullein, Periwinkle, Raspberry, Shepherd's Purse.

DIGESTION, Aids to: Angelica, Allspice, Anise, Arrowroot, Balm, Caraway, Cardamom, Centaury, Cinnamon, Dandelion, Dill, Elecampane, Fennel, Golden Rod, Ground Ivy, Horseradish, Hyssop, Juniper, Marjoram, Meadowsweet, Mint, Nettle, Parsley, Pepper, Periwinkle, Red Clover, Quassia, Sage, Salad Burnet, Savory, Slippery Elm, Turmeric, Verbena.

DISINFECTANT: Peppers, Golden Rod, Goosegrass, Lavender, Rosemary, Sage, Wormwood.

DIURETIC: Bay, Belladonna, Dandelion, Elder, Elecampane, Foxglove, Garlic, Germander, Golden Rod, Ground Elder, Groundsel, Hawthorn, Horehound, Horseradish, Horsetail, Juniper, Ladies' Bedstraw, Lily-of-the-Valley, Mistletoe, Mugwort, Mustard, Nasturtium, Nettle, Pansy, Parsley, Plantain, Shallot, Sorrel, Uva-ursi, Woodruff.

EARACHE: Poppy.
Excessive earwax: Agrimony.

ECZEMA: Chickweed, Golden Rod.

EMPHYSEMA: Nasturtium.

EPILEPSY: Mistletoe, Skullcap, Valerian.

EXPECTORANT: Lobelia.

EYES (conjunctivitis, etc.): Centaury, Chickweed, Eyebright, Fennel, Golden Rod, Lovage, Marshmallow, Melilot, Plantain, Rosemary, Rue (cataracts).

FEVER: Aconite, Couch grass, Fenugreek, Garlic, Hyssop, Plantain, Purslane.

FLATULENCE: Angelica, Cardamom, Catmint, Centaury, Ginger, Juniper, Lovage, Melilot, Nutmeg, Pepper, Rue, Tarragon, Valerian.

GOUT: Ground Elder (poultice), Lime flowers, Male Fern (poultice), Soapwort.

HAY FEVER: Eyebright, Mullein.

HEADACHE: Allspice, Balm, Lavender, Rosemary, Valerian, Vervain, Violet.

HEART: Aconite (sedative), Foxglove, Hawthorn, Lily-of-the-Valley, Motherwort, Rosemary (palpitation), Soapwort.

HEMORRHAGE: Peppers, Comfrey (internal), Golden Rod, Horsetail (internal and external), Nettle, Periwinkle, Plantain (external), Saffron (internal), Shepherd's Purse (nose-bleed), Yarrow (nose-bleed and profuse bleeding after confinement or tooth extraction). HICCUPS: Dill, Mint, Mustard, Wood Betony.

INSECT BITES and STINGS: Arrowroot, Costmary, Fennel, Feverfew, Gentian, Hyssop, Marigold, Parsley, Plantain, Savory.

INSOMNIA: Goosegrass, Hawthorn, Hops, Ladies' Slipper, Marjoram, Melilot, Mullein, Nutmeg, Valerian.

JAUNDICE: Alfalfa, Soapwort.

KIDNEYS

Poor function: Alfalfa, Golden Rod, Ground Ivy, Lime flowers, Lovage, Parsley.

Stones or gravel: Golden Rod, Ladies' Bedstraw, Nettle, Parsley Piert, Sesame, Shepherd's Purse, Yarrow.

LACTATION

To increase: Alfalfa, Anise, Blessed Thistle, Dill, Fennel, Fenugreek, Marshmallow.

To dry up: Sage.

LIVER: Cascara Sagrada, Dandelion, Fennel, Gentian, Golden Rod, Horehound, Hyssop, Lime flowers, Lobelia, Marigold, Poke Root (spleen), Rhubarb, Rosemary, Uva-ursi (spleen),

lavender—and what could look more exotic than a scattering of marigold petals? The list could go on. A single herb or a mixture, well chopped, can be added to a plain French dressing, or beaten into butter and soft cheese, and a sprig of mint or borage does wonders for a fruit drink. A plain vegetable can be made into something special if served with a scattering of chopped fresh herbs over it. Seeds are useful here too. Everyone will have a favorite so there is no point in being arbitrary, but some flavors suit some vegetables better than others. Here are some good combinations.

BEANS (green) — summer savory, marjoram, sage, dill seeds.

BEETS — fresh basil, caraway, coriander and fennel seeds.

CABBAGE — fresh mint and lovage, caraway and fennel seeds.

CARROTS — fresh mint, parsley, thyme, basil, sesame seeds, allspice.

ONIONS — fresh sage, tarragon, thyme.

Vervain, Woodruff, Wormwood, Yarrow.

LUMBAGO: Juniper, Vervain (both poultices).

LUNGS: Chickweed, Comfrey, Marshmallow, Mullein, Slippery Elm. MENOPAUSE: Mugwort.

MENSTRUAL DIFFICULTIES: Balm, Chamomile (pre-menstrual tension), Costmary, Gentian, Germander, Ground Ivy, Groundsel, Hops, Ladies' Mantle (excessive), Melilot, Motherwort, Mugwort, Nettle, Parsley, Pasque Flower (pre-menstrual tension), Pennyroyal, Raspberry, Rue, Saffron, Shepherd's Purse (excessive flow with pain), Southernwood, Valerian, Vervain, Yarrow.

MIGRAINE: Fennel, Fenugreek, Pasque Flower, Thyme, Valerian.

NAUSEA: Cloves, Pennyroyal.

NERVES:

Exhaustion: Pansy, Pennyroyal. Food: Red Clover, Sage, Violet.
Sedative: Belladonna, Chamomile, Cowslip, Evening Primrose, Ground Elder, Hawthorn, Hemlock, Hops, Lavender, Ladies' Bedstraw, Ladies' Slipper, Lime flowers, Mugwort, Nutmeg, Pasque Flower, Skullcap, Valerian, Verbena, Vervain, Wood Betony.
Stimulant: Ginseng. Sudorific: Poppy.

NEURALGIA: Aconite, Catmint, Feverfew, Vervain.

NIGHTMARE: Rosemary.

PAIN RELIEF: Peppers, Elderflowers, Hops, Meadowsweet, Melilot, Valerian.

PERSPIRATION:

Bringing on: Angelica, Balm, Elderflowers, Elecampane, Garlic, Germander, Ginger, Groundsel, Horseradish, Juniper, Lime flowers, Marigold, Meadowsweet, Mustard, Pennyroyal, Saffron, Thistle (Blessed), Yarrow
Checking: Myrtle.

PILES: Cascara Sagrada, Catmint, Elder, Lesser Celandine, Plantain, Solomon's Seal, Witch-hazel.

SINUS: Elderflowers, Horseradish, Plantain, Rosemary.

SKIN: Burdock, Golden Rod (eczema and psoriasis), Chickweed, Golden Rod, Poke Root.

SORE THROAT: Bergamot, Hawthorn, Mullein, Raspberry (vinegar), Sage, Thyme.

STIMULANT: Peppers, Caraway, Cloves, Germander, Ginger, Horseradish, Hyssop, Lobelia, Marjoram, Mustard, Nettle, Rosemary, Southernwood.

SUNBURN and SUNSTROKE: Aloe, Salad Burnet.

TONIC: Angelica root, Agrimony, Borage, Caraway, Chervil, Chickweed, Costmary, Dandelion, Eyebright, Fenugreek, Flax, Gentian, Germander, Ginseng, Goosegrass, Ground Ivy, Hops, Horehound, Horseradish, Ladies' Slipper, Lily-of-the Valley, Marjoram, Motherwort, Mugwort, Nettle, Periwinkle, Purslane, Quassia, Rosemary, Salad Burnet, Sorrel, Southernwood, Sweet Cicely, Thistle (Blessed), Thyme, Woodruff, Wormwood.

TONSILLITIS: Comfrey, Fenugreek, Slippery Elm.

TOOTHACHE: Allspice, Cloves, Marjoram, Mint, Poppy.

ULCERS: Aloe, Chickweed, Comfrey (stomach), Golden Rod, Golden Seal, Licorice (stomach), Marigold, Sage (mouth), St. John's Wort, Slippery Elm, Vervain.

URINATION:
Cleansing: Pansy, Parsley Piert, Uva-ursi.
Painful: St. John's Wort.
Suppressed: Catmint, Fennel, Foxglove, Gentian, Juniper, Ladies' Bedstraw, Rosemary.

UTERINE BLEEDING: Saffron.

UTERINE CANCER: Red Clover.

VAGINAL DISORDERS: Golden Rod, Ladies' Mantle, Lavender, Thistle (Blessed), Uva-ursi.

VARICOSE VEINS: Melilot.

PEAS — fresh mint, tarragon, sorrel.

POTATOES — fresh basil, chives, mint, parsley, fennel, sage, rosemary.

SPINACH — fresh marjoram, mint, sorrel.

TOMATOES — fresh basil, marjoram, sage, allspice.

Lettuce is not the only salad base—young dandelion leaves, blanched chicory, Florentine fennel, lovage and sorrel can all be used.

Ulcerated: Agrimony, Marigold, Yarrow.

VOMITING:

To induce: Mustard, Poke Root.

To reduce: Mint, Nutmeg, Raspberry.

WARTS: Dandelion, Greater Celandine.

WHOOPING COUGH: Evening Primrose, Lobelia, Mistletoe, Pennyroyal, Red Clover, Violet.

WORMS, Expulsion of: Aloe, Garlic, Gentian, Horehound, Hyssop, Male Fern, Mugwort, Nettle, Plantain, Rue, Senna, Southernwood, Vervain, Wormwood.

WOUNDS: Agrimony, Aloe, Arrowroot, Comfrey, Golden Rod, Ladies' Mantle, Marigold, Marshmallow, Meadowsweet, Pansy, Parsley, Rosemary, St. John's Wort, Slippery Elm, Thyme, Vervain, Yarrow.

Slow to heal: German Chamomile, Solomon's Seal, Witch-hazel, Yarrow.

Medicinal Herbs and Spices for Composite Treatment

By taking a mixture of herbs, an illness can be tackled on several fronts at once and, since some herbs can act as a catalyst on others, increase their efficacy. A qualified herbalist will offer wider advice than can be given here and should be consulted whenever a condition has become really troublesome. The following recipes should be treated as suggestions and not specifics.

ARTHRITIS — Mix equal quantities of couch grass root, meadowsweet and marjoram with half the quantity of coltsfoot. Use as a tea. Or mix equal quantities elder leaves, golden rod and rosemary with half the quantity of coltsfoot.

ASTHMA — Asthma and hay fever are, in some quarters, regarded as an indication that the body is not making enough use of the potassium provided in the food taken or that not enough potassium is being provided. Herbs that contain potassium and that can be drunk alone or in combination as an alternative to the conventional "tea" are coltsfoot, comfrey, fennel seed, mistletoe, mullein, yarrow.

BLOOD PRESSURE (high) – Catmint, mint, skullcap and valerian tea.

BRONCHITIS – Boil up a healthy quantity of red clover flowers with some flax seed. Add honey and lemon juice and drink while hot.

COLDS – Mint and yarrow tea. Elderflower and mint tea.

CONSTIPATION – Mix together equal quantities mint, marjoram and senna leaves, add one-third quantity chamomile flowers. Use as a tea.

ECZEMA – Mix equal quantities violet leaves and senna pods with a lesser quantity meadowsweet and a dash of juniper berries. Use as a tea. Mix equal quantities chamomile flowers, marshmallow, marigold flowers, sage leaves and vervain. Make into a tea and use as a lotion.

HEADACHE – Catmint, mint, skullcap and valerian—equal quantities. Use as a tea. Chamomile flowers and mint leaves. Ground ivy, feverfew, rosemary, wood betony.

HICCUPS – Mint and wood betony. Use as a tea and sip slowly.

INSOMNIA – Balm and marjoram with a lesser quantity anise and valerian. Mix well and use as a bedtime tea. Equal quantities hops, skullcap and valerian. If valerian gives the tea a taste you don't like, sweeten it with honey. Mint with half the quantity rue and wood betony.

KIDNEYS – Equal quantities chamomile flowers, dandelion, juniper berries, parsley and uva-ursi. Use as a tea.

LACTATION – Equal quantities anise, basil, fennel, nettle and vervain. Use as a tea.

LIVER – Equal quantities angelica, chamomile flowers, dandelion, gentian, golden rod, horsetail, parsley and thistle (blessed). Use as a tea. If assembling all the ingredients is impossible, use as many as you can find.

LUNGS – Equal quantities comfrey, marshmallow, mullein and slippery elm with some lobelia. Use as a tea. Equal quantities chickweed, comfrey, marshmallow and mullein. Use as a tea.

MENSTRUAL DIFFICULTIES — Equal quantities chamomile flowers, mugwort, rosemary, sage and shepherd's purse. Use as a tea.

MIGRAINE — Fenugreek and thyme tea.

NERVES — Valerian and mint with some chamomile and lavender flowers use as a tea. Mint leaves with a lesser quantity anise, hops and horsetail and flowers. Use as a tea. PAIN — Any severe continuing pain should be referred to a doctor. As a temporary measure, try a tea made from equal quantities balm, elderflowers, hawthorn leaves, lavender flowers and St. John's Wort. VOMITING — Severe and continued vomiting is again a case for professional attention. In simple cases try a tea made from equal quantities balm, chamomile flowers, centaury, fennel seed and mint.

WATER — When the body is carrying too much water, a simple diuretic tea can be made using equal quantities juniper berries, horsetail, nettle, rosemary and yarrow.

Cooking with Herbs and Spices

There is more to cooking with herbs and spices than just throwing a handful into the pot and hoping for the best. If you use too many different ones together and add them to a stew at the beginning of cooking time, you will not be pleased with the result. There is quite an art in using herbs as food flavoring; enough of them should be used to bring out the flavor of the food but not so much that all one can taste is the herb. Heat releases the volatile oils they contain and too much of it can taste bitter; a random collection of herbs can release oils which war with each other taste-wise.

Since fresh herbs are not available all the year round, there has to be a dependence on dried or frozen ones. Some herbs freeze better than others and, when defrosted, can only be used in cooking as they become too limp for use in salads or as a garnish. Home-dried herbs are usually preferable to bought ones, which are often sold in clear-glass bottles (which does the herb contained no good at all) and who is to say how long they have been sitting on the shelf? When you do buy dried herbs, as most of us must at some time, buy the smallest amount possible. Spices, bought ground, seem to keep their flavor better but, if you can, buy whole spices and seeds and grind them just before use. I keep a special pepper grinder for seeds and depend on a fine grater for spices, such as nutmeg.

The use of herbs and spices in cooking is nowhere near as widespread or prevalent as it could be. Mint sauce, parsley sauce, sage and onion stuffing and a dusting of nutmeg on a milk pudding is as far as many people go and even constant herb-users often do not realize that their favorite herbs can be used in more ways than the well-tried ones.

Here are suggestions for use.

ALFALFA SOUP
see "Alfalfa," Medicinal Herb section

ALLSPICE
Allspice, a single spice, which has the composite flavors of nutmeg, cloves and cinnamon, can be bought whole or ground. Good sprinkled over plain steamed fish; add a pinch to lemon and thyme stuffing for chicken; mix with a little sugar for use with tart fruits; add to apples made into a pie; add to scone and cake mixtures; use instead of powdered nutmeg for dusting over egg custard and rice puddings, etc.

ANGELICA

ANGELICA LIQUEUR
see "Angelica," Medicinal Herb section

CANDIED ANGELICA
see "Angelica," Medicinal Herb section

ANISE
The bruised seeds taste good in applesauce and fish soup.

BALM

The light minty-lemon taste of the leaves is very pleasant in a salad and gives a clean tang to stuffings used for greasy meats.

Always include a few leaves in a punch that relies on a red wine as its base.

BASIL

Apart from the mandatory sprinkling of chopped basil leaves over sliced tomatoes, it can also be used in the making of sauces. See "Basil," Medicinal Herb section for the recipe for the famous Pesto Sauce.

A plain tomato soup, or better still, a tomato and onion soup, can be thickened and made more exciting by the last-minute addition of yogurt or cottage cheese and some chopped basil. Beat the cheese before adding to remove the lumps and heat the mixture gently to encourage the basil leaves to release their flavor. Do not boil. This soup can be served either hot or cold.

BAY

Just one bay leaf will give a milk pudding or custard a better flavor. Milk in which bay leaves have been soaking will make a bland white sauce take on more character. Try a leaf in the vegetable cooking water.

BERGAMOT

The clean sharp taste of bergamot makes the chopped leaves a pleasant inclusion in a salad and the pretty red flowers make a nice garnish.

The leaves give an uninteresting white wine a decided "lift."

BORAGE

The cucumber-like taste of the leaves makes them a good inclusion in salads. The flowers make an edible garnish.

CARAWAY

The spicy taste of the seeds is good in soups and savory dishes and a pinch in the water in which green vegetables are cooking will often overcome the prejudices of finicky children.

If you would like the flavor in a sauce but not the seeds, soak the bruised seeds in a little hot water and, when strained, use that with the milk or other liquid for the sauce.

The seeds can be added to the mixture for cakes and scones. For Seed Cake recipe see "Caraway," Medicinal Herb section.

CARDAMOM

If you make your own curry powder, be sure to use cardamom. The seedpods can be bought whole and you can remove the seeds and grind them yourself to make a more pungent flavoring than the bought ground cardamom which, I am told, contains the seedpods too.

Some people love the flavor of cardamom, others don't seem to like it at all, so it will be as well to check with the family before using it sprinkled over fruit salads and fruit pies, or taking the trouble to make a cardamom syrup. This is made by simmering an equal mixture of honey and water with lemon juice and some ground cardamom seed.

For the recipe for Cardamom Carrots see "Cardamom," Medicinal Herb section.

CHERVIL

Chervil has a curious flavor somewhere between parsley and anise, but it is clean and fresh and tastes very good with almost everything but sweet dishes. Use it chopped over salads, in mayonnaise, French dressing, beaten into the eggs for an omelet, into butter and soft cheese, and over vegetables just before serving.

For recipes for a simple Chervil Sauce and Chervil Soup see "Chervil," Medicinal Herb section.

CHIVES

Wherever you would like a mild onion flavor, use freshly chopped chives. In salads, soups, sauces, with vegetables, egg and cheese dishes, etc.

CINNAMON

Cinnamon can be used for both savory and sweet dishes. Pumpkin, which can be too bland for some people, tastes much more interesting when a little cinnamon powder is beaten into the mash.

A little cinnamon powder will "cut" the grease of pork and other chops and enliven bland stewed fruit, plain puddings and junkets. It is a well-known cake spice and the "sticks" (the thin curling quills of the bark of the tree) are often added to pickling vinegar and fruit and wine punches.

The recipes for Cinnamon Toast and a quick, delicious and very simple sweet can be found in the Medicinal Herb section under "Cinnamon."

CLOVES

There is a whole generation resistant to the flavor of cloves. In the old days when toothache was part of childhood, a whole clove would be plugged into an aching tooth to take away the pain so, for older members of the community there is little pleasure to be found in that strange, distinctive flavor. But for a palate that comes to it fresh and unburdened with memories, there is pleasure to be found in the clove.

Try it with beets, either cooked or raw; in potato soup or with stewed pears or in an apple pie. Ground cloves can be added to the mixture for cakes and biscuits, stuffings, sauces, pickles and marinades.

Stud an orange with cloves and add it to the water in which you boil a piece of bacon, or stud an onion with cloves and add that to the water in which you boil a chicken.

A ham for baking can be deeply scored in a diamond pattern and studded with cloves, cherries and pineapple. A leg of lamb, plugged with cloves and given a sprinkling of sugar and chopped marjoram leaves, makes a gourmet dish.

CORIANDER

Coriander seeds can be bought either whole or ground. It has a faintly nutmeg-like flavor. The seeds can be used whole or bruised and go well with sharp citrus flavors. A lemon or orange marmalade tastes lively and spicy when coriander seeds are added. Just put a little muslin bag of well-bruised seeds in with the peel, etc. when boiling up and before the sugar is added for the final boil. The bag is easily removed.

A humble apple crumble becomes a gourmet dish when crushed coriander seed mixed with a little sugar is spread on top of the crumble before baking.

CUMIN

Cumin seed is another that should always be added to homemade curry powder. The flavor is warm rather than hot but quite definite.

A few crushed seeds tossed into the water in which cabbage or beans are cooked give the vegetables a good flavor, and the crushed seeds rubbed into lamb or beef before roasting help the meat flavor. A thick tomato sauce flavored with bruised cumin seeds also makes a good "meat-rub." Try it with meat cooked on the barbecue.

Add cumin seed to canned soups to give distinction.

DILL and FENNEL

The taste of dill and fennel is so similar they can be considered in tandem. The young leaves of both plants can be used chopped in salads; fennel leaves are good with fish.

The fat stem of Florentine fennel can be used whole as a vegetable or grated. The seeds of both plants are very tasty in soups, sauces, etc. See "Dill" and "Fennel" in the Medicinal Herb section for further information.

FENUGREEK

Fenugreek seeds are often found in curry powders. The sprouted seed that has considerable food value can be eaten raw. It is slightly bitter but the sprouts taste good mixed with left-over mashed potatoes and fried or, mixed smooth and let down with milk and given plenty of black pepper as seasoning, make a nourishing soup.

GARLIC

Rubbed round the salad bowl or the saucepan in which vegetables are to be cooked, added, minced, to soups, sauces, meat and chicken dishes, garlic can give a flavor that makes the dish for some people and renders it inedible to others. You are either a garlic or non-garlic person.

For recipes for Garlic Bread, Garlic Soup and Garlic Sauce see "Garlic," Medicinal Herb section.

GERANIUM, ROSE

The sweetly-scented leaves of rose geranium give jellies, junket, stewed fruit and egg custard a clean and unusual flavor. Try them chopped and beaten into cream cheese or yogurt.

For the recipe for Rose Geranium Jelly, see "Geranium," Medicinal Herb section.

GINGER

You can buy ginger fresh or powdered. The fresh root is an essential ingredient of Chinese dishes. The powder is used in cakes and biscuits and some savory recipes—if you like the flavor, experiment with a touch of it with meat and fish. The root can be pickled, candied and used to make ginger beer. Candied ginger makes a lovely filling for homemade chocolates.

HAWTHORN

For jelly, see "Hawthorn," Medicinal Herb section.

HOREHOUND

For recipes for Horehound Beer and Horehound Toffee, see "Horehound," Medicinal Herb section.

HORSERADISH

In addition to the recipe for Horseradish Sauce in the Medicinal Herb section under "Horseradish," here is a composite recipe for sauce and vinegar.

JUNIPER

Crushed juniper berries are good added to sauerkraut and coleslaw. Try a few at a time to get the flavor right for you. Stuffings, particularly for game birds, hare, rabbit, duck, goose and turkey, are better when a few crushed berries are included.

The stewed berries, well-sweetened, make a delicious side-of-the-plate-type condiment for greasy dishes.

LAVENDER

Lavender vinegar and lavender sugar are both very simply made. Just pack lavender flowers in a bottle of white vinegar and leave in a warm place for a week or two. The strained vinegar is delicious with a plain salad.

A few flowers left in the sugar container will scent the sugar slightly. Good for the top of a plain sponge cake.

LOVAGE

Lovage with its celery taste is good added, well-chopped, to salads and sprinkled over green vegetables before serving. It goes well with fish and chicken dishes. Lovage stems can be candied.

See "Lovage," Medicinal Herb section for the recipe for Potato and Lovage Soup.

MARIGOLD

The fresh petals can be added to salads and fruit salads. The dried petals give flavor to homemade cottage cheese, soups and stews.

MARJORAM

The finely chopped leaves are good with salads, egg, fish, meat and poultry dishes. Try marjoram instead of sage when making an onion stuffing to go with liver or sausage dishes.

The blander-tasting vegetables are improved by the addition of marjoram as are plain cheese scones. Dried marjoram, well-seasoned, can be rubbed over poultry before roasting.

Marjoram vinegar makes a change from tarragon vinegar. It can be made with either the fresh or dried herb.

MEADOWSWEET

A good source of Vitamin C, both flowers and leaves can be added to homemade beers to give added nourishment. A simple and pleasant drink can be made by simmering the leaves for about half an hour and then adding sugar to the strained liquid.

MINT

The chopped leaves can be added to salads, fruit salads, soups (particularly cold ones), soft cheeses, fish, lamb and veal dishes, vegetables, salad dressings, split-pea dishes, savory pancakes, marmalades, fruit drinks and hot punch. Try apple or orange mint with peas and carrots.

Mint vinegar made by infusing the leaves in white vinegar for a fortnight and then straining is good to use with olive oil as a French dressing.

Recipes for Mint Sauce and Mint Jelly can be found under "Mint," Medicinal Herb section.

MUSTARD

For recipes for Smooth and Nutty Mustards see "Mustard," Medicinal Herb section.

NASTURTIUM

The fiery-tasting leaves are good in salads. The seeds can be used instead of capers. They are good pickled. A white sauce can be enlivened by the addition of a few very finely chopped seeds cooked with it.

For recipe for Nasturtium Vinegar, etc., see "Nasturtium," Medicinal Herb section.

NETTLE

For recipe for Nettle Beer see "Nettle," Medicinal Herb section.

NUTMEG

Nutmeg is best used freshly grated from the whole nut. Use sprinkled over cooked vegetables (particularly potatoes, carrots and cauliflower), rice puddings, egg custards, stewed fruit, fruit salads, hot milk at bedtime and puddings (particularly bread pudding).

Some people like the flavor in meat loaf, omelets and scrambled eggs.

PARSLEY

Parsley should be eaten—not just left on the side of the plate—when used as a garnish. The whole sprig can put people off but they are more likely to eat it when it is finely chopped.

Salads, soups, vegetables, fish, meat, poultry, egg and cheese dishes can all be served with a sprinkling of parsley. It is good in sauces (who does not know parsley sauce?), beaten, well-chopped into butter, soft cheese and pâtes.

PEPPER

Black peppercorns and green peppercorns can both be used to make pepper steaks. The black peppercorns should be well bruised before using as a coating for both sides of the steak. You can, if you like, thump them into the steak with the flat side of a Chinese chopper. Leave the steak to stand for at least one hour before cooking to allow the flavor of the peppers to be absorbed by the meat. The Chinese brush steak with soy sauce well laced with garlic before adding the peppers.

Green peppercorns can be tucked into pockets made on each side of a steak before frying. Peg the pockets tight with toothpicks. A mixture of crushed green peppercorns, crushed garlic and a dash of lemon juice can be added to butter spread over a steak before cooking.

POPPY SEEDS

You can rely on bought poppy seeds as being non-narcotic. They are delicious toasted in a dry frying pan over low heat. Keep them well tossed. Spread over a baking sheet and left in a moderate oven for 10-15 minutes, they will toast equally well.

You can roll homemade sweets in them, sprinkle them over bread rolls, scones, pasta, pastries, grilled fish and new potatoes. Cottage cheese and parsley and cream cheese and parsley made into balls and rolled in poppy seeds are delicious.

Poppy seed cake is not the most flavorsome of cakes but is worth a try. The seed must be left soaking in milk for at least an hour—longer is better.

RASPBERRY

For recipes for Raspberry Jam and Raspberry Vinegar see "Raspberry," Medicinal Herb section.

RHUBARB

For recipes for Rhubarb and Ginger Jam and Rhubarb Wine—or at least a variation of it—see "Rhubarb," Medicinal Herb section.

ROSEMARY

Rosemary is a pungent herb and its leaves are tough; there is quite a strong argument for its use dried rather than fresh. The powdered herb can be used scattered over soups, cooked vegetables, most meat dishes, cheese and egg dishes, etc.

You can make rosemary sugar by leaving a few sprigs in the sugar container for a time and rosemary vinegar by steeping the flowers in wine vinegar. A sprig of flowers can be candied.

The oils contained in the leaves help digestion of fatty meats such as young lamb and pork chops. Slit the meat and tuck in a few leaves before grilling. Add well-chopped rosemary leaves to onion sauce used with these meats.

Rosemary is good in sweet dishes too. Add a dash of powdered rosemary to the apples for apple pie or to the milk for egg custard. Plain cheese scones are given added bite by the addition of a little powdered rosemary.

The best use I have found for rosemary, though, is with baked potatoes. Brush the cut side of the potatoes with salt in which dried rosemary has been mixed and bake with a leg of lamb.

SAFFRON

Saffron has a light flavor but the color is wonderful. See "Saffron," Medicinal Herb section for recipes for Fish Soup, Paella and Saffron Cake.

SAGE

Sage has a strong clean flavor and is good to use either fresh or dried. Use it sprinkled over cooked vegetables, fish soup, cooked fish and meats, stews, etc. It is particularly good used in stuffings with onions for use with fatty meats.

As an accompaniment to fatty meats try sage fritters. Dip the leaves in batter and drop into hot oil until the batter is crisp. A green jelly with the addition of well-chopped sage leaves can be poured into an ice-cube tray and allowed to set for use with a liver dish.

Rub meat joints with a bruised sage leaf before roasting. Add sage to a white sauce; make sage vinegar for use with salads by steeping the leaves in white vinegar; add chopped sage leaves to butter for serving with steaks; beat chopped sage leaves into homemade cheese or bought cream and cottage cheese. Add them to yogurt to make a quick salad dressing. Sage leaves, added to a plain scone or a cheese scone mixture, give added flavor.

SALAD BURNET

The fresh leaves give a cucumber-like taste to salads, butter, cream and cottage cheese, and fruit drinks.

SUMMER SAVORY

The sweet peppery flavor of summer savory is at its best when used with bean dishes as it brings out the flavor of the beans without swamping it with its own individual taste. Use a sprinkling of the herb with frozen or canned green beans, butter beans, etc.

If on a salt-free diet, use chopped summer savory as a vegetable flavoring. Use it on fish and meat dishes, stuffings, coleslaws and sauerkraut, soups and sauces.

SESAME SEEDS
Use roasted, sprinkled over cakes and biscuits, salads and vegetables.

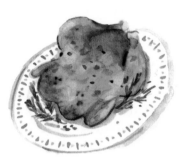

SHALLOTS
Use the leaves chopped, in salads, added to soups, casseroles, rice, meat and chicken dishes.

SORREL
The sharp lemony bitter taste of sorrel leaves may or may not recommend themselves for use in salads. Cooked and added to a white sauce or blanched and added to an omelet they could find favor.

SUNFLOWER
Sunflower seeds, husked, can be added to salads and fruit salads as a valuable food. See "Sunflower," Medicinal Herb section for recipes for a sunflower drink and Sunflower Toffee.

SWEET CICELY
Try the roots stir-fried and the leaves candied.

TARRAGON
Tarragon can be used both fresh and dried. Fresh is best. It has a sharpish taste that goes well with chicken and fish dishes, omelets, asparagus and carrots. The chopped leaves are good added to mayonnaise, tomato salads, creamed mushrooms and sauces. The well-known Tartare, Hollandaise and Bearnaise sauces all taste better if tarragon is included.

THYME

Garden thyme can be used either alone or in a bouquet garni with meat and chicken dishes, in soups, stuffings, sauces, pickles, marinades, etc. and is one of the most widely used and best-loved herbs whether fresh or dried. Cooked beans, beets, eggplants, marrow, mushrooms, potatoes, onions and zucchini all taste better when given a sprinkling of the fresh chopped herb and even dry, it does not come amiss.

As with most of the other herbs, it blends well with cream and cottage cheese and butter. Pancakes with thyme butter and runny honey are delicious. Savory scones and herb breads need thyme. Lemon thyme is very good with stewed apples.

TURMERIC

The powdered root is mostly used to give color to mustard pickles and curry powder.

VERBENA

Use the leaves to give a lemony flavor to fish dishes, fruit drinks, jams and jellies.

VIOLET

The little flowers can be candied and used as an edible decoration. Just dip them in well-beaten white of egg and dip in fine sugar and allow to dry slowly. Store in a tightly-closed container.

HERB COMBINATIONS

Herbs can be used alone or in company with others; some herbs complement each other and make good bedfellows. The famous bouquet garni is a case in point. The composition of it varies from cook to cook but it is always used in the same way; if the herbs are fresh, they are tied together by the stems and allowed to hang by the cotton that ties them into the food that is being cooked. At the end of cooking time they are retrieved and discarded. Dried herbs are tied up in a bit of muslin or fine cloth and are similarly removed when cooking is over.

A bouquet garni can be as simple as a bay leaf, some sprigs of parsley and some of thyme. Another version is a sprig each of thyme, marjoram and chervil, a few stalks of parsley and chives and one bay leaf and one sage leaf. Yet another can be made from dried herbs in equal quantities parsley with chives with half the amount thyme and lovage.

Since few herbs actually swear at each other from a flavor point of view, there is obviously scope for experimentation and personal choice. But it pays to have some knowledge of which herbs go best with sweet dishes and which are best with savory ones. Sweet herbs would do nothing for a greasy meat dish. Just as herbs can be mixed, so can spices. Cinnamon, cardamom and cloves go particularly well together.

If you dry your own herbs, you can store them separately and then use some of each when cooking, but a quicker way is to make the mixture when you collect and dry your herbs at the end of summer and store that. Herbs are such generous providers it is not worthwhile drying too many of them at a time—the next crop is too often waiting to be dried long before the last season's one has been used.

HERE ARE A FEW SUGGESTED HERB COMBINATIONS

Fish — chives, dill and parsley; marjoram, thyme, basil, fennel.

Chicken (in stuffings) — parsley, chives, marjoram, lovage and a few juniper berries; chives, marjoram, basil, thyme, lovage, parsley; sage and chives with some grated lemon peel.

Egg and cheese dishes — parsley, dill, tarragon, lovage, chives.

Meat stews — parsley, chives with a lesser amount marjoram, lovage, tarragon and thyme.

Lamb and veal dishes — marjoram, rosemary, summer savory.

Meat dishes, fried, roasted or barbecued — parsley, chives, tarragon, thyme.

Pork dishes — sage and basil.

Vegetables — almost any combination but the sweet herbs.

If you don't have lovage, use a snipping of celery leaves instead, but go carefully as the flavor can be harsh.

The lemon-flavored thymes, mints and balms go well with sweet cicely for sweet dishes.

Oils

Just as one keeps a few cloves of garlic steeping in oil for use with salads, green herbs can be used too, but they have to be treated a little more carefully. The more aromatic herbs such as basil, thyme and rosemary are the best ones to use.

Bruise the leaves well, place in a glass jar and cover with a tasteless oil. Cover lightly, and keep in a warm place for at least a fortnight giving the contents a good stir every day. If you use a wooden spoon, you can press the herbs to get as much oil released as possible. Strain, pressing as you go. Bottle and seal.

These oils can be used to coat meat before grilling, roasting or barbecuing, with fish and poultry in the same way, in marinades and dressings, etc. A light coating on the frying pan in which you make savory pancakes will improve their flavor. Try an oil in place of margarine or butter when making savory scones.

Herbs for fragrance

MAKING POTPOURRI

"Potpourri," that delightful word so evocative of the sensual pleasure of a drift of fragrance on the air, has such pleasant connotations that it is often forgotten that it actually means "rotted pot," a name derived from the French verb "pourrir" which means "to grow rotten." The name came about by reason of the method once used to retain the fragrance of flowers and herbs. The "moist method," as it is called, is seldom used today, largely, one imagines, because the result, while certainly fragrant, has no eye-appeal and the "dry method" has both.

I read recently that "potpourri" was also a culinary term for a thick stew made from bits of leftover meat and vegetables. Whoever coined the term was certainly giving his opinion of it!

In the days when the "moist method" was used, roses had a fragrance seldom found in our modern varieties, and time, it seems, did not press so heavily. How seldom, we find a garden drenched with the scent of the great, pink cabbage roses, or the many-petalled damask rose as so many gardens were just a few generations back. To get a real rose scent today you have to shop around; the roses with the strongest perfume seem to be the single, dark-red ones.

Rose petals and lavender flowers have always been popular choices for potpourri because they have the ability to retain their fragrance for a long time without the help of "fixatives." They should always be considered as the "base" of the mixture.

THE MOIST METHOD

Buy plenty of common rock salt. Sea salt will do but it comes expensive. Bought packet salt will not do.

Find a large, pleasant-looking crock. As the year goes by and the flowers and herbs in your garden come into bloom, make a morning foray and gather a picking of scented flowers and leaves. (Rose, lavender, verbena, bergamot, marjoram, carnation, rosemary, mignonette, etc.) Only gather enough to make a layer in your pot after the flowers and leaves have been left for about two days to wilt. They do not have to become dry, just raddled-looking.

Make a layer of your batch in the crock, sprinkle it with crumbled rock salt, add another layer, sprinkle that with the salt. Put a plate on the mixture, press it down, and weight it with whatever you have to hand. I use the old weights from a discarded grandfather clock. Keep on in this way until either your crock is full or your harvest is at an end; press the mixture down, cover, weight, and forget for a few weeks.

Some recipes advocate stirring the mixture as each addition of salt is made; others make no mention of stirring. Since you are likely to find a dark liquid has collected at the bottom of the crock you may think, as I do, that it should be stirred through the mixture to enable as much of it as possible to be absorbed.

The object of the exercise is to produce a "cake" which is evenly damp-dry and which holds the full fragrance contained in the flowers and leaves of the mixture. After a few weeks, the "cake" will be ready.

You can use it as it is, broken up, and the pieces put into the type of jar that has a perforated lid and so allows the fragrance to escape; you will need to give the "cake" a good prod every now and then. Choose as pretty a jar as possible and keep the "cake" out of sight. Or you can break up the "cake" and mix it with some spices and orrisroot and powdered orange or lemon peel with a dash of brandy to act as a preservative. The orrisroot and peel are the fixatives and don't be tempted to use the peel just dried and grated; if you are not prepared to take the trouble to dry and powder it, forget it and just use the orrisroot.

If you can steel yourself and use half a cup of brandy instead of the dash, so much the better. Mix the ingredients well, then put them back into the crock, cover and weigh down and leave for at least six months. This makes a superior potpourri with a very long-lasting scent. The look of it may not please you, but the fragrance certainly will and anyone with the interest and patience to have got this far will surely find a personal inventive way of using the product.

THE DRY METHOD

This enables the color of the flowers to give pleasure as well as the scent. First, collect a number of screw-topped jars.

Then, in an empty, airy room or any other suitable place, up-end an old chair and, using a large square of muslin or similarly porous material, tie a corner to each of the four legs to make a tray. Air will be able to pass both above and below the suspended material.

As the year goes by collect scented flowers and leaves and spread them on the material to dry, keeping each variety separate. The collection is best made in the morning, after the dew has dried and before the sun has become hot. As each pile dries and becomes crisp, store it in one of the screw-topped jars and label.

Keep on going right through the summer, filling up the jars. Discard any flowers and leaves that have turned brown—the flowers should keep their red, yellow or violet colors, etc. (White flowers have a tendency to turn a dingy yellow-brown so, no matter how sweetly scented, don't depend on them). The number of jars you use is up to you; the choice of scents is up to you. Bay, jasmine and frangipani (watch these two), violets, rose petals, lavender and rosemary flowers and leaves, marigold petals, port-wine magnolia flowers, carnation petals, mint leaves, marjoram, verbena flowers and leaves, can all be used and there is no need to make the same mixture twice; that is one of the lovely things about a potpourri—you can do it your way and hardly go wrong however you do it. Chamomile, costmary, woodruff, scented-leaved geranium, mignonette, bergamot, plumbago flowers, forget-me-nots, cornflowers, orange-red nasturtium flowers—you can choose for color as well as for scent.

When you are ready, assemble your jars and a large mixing bowl.

Mix your ingredients in any proportion that pleases you and stir well by hand, taking a good sniff every now and then and distributing the colors evenly through the mixture.

Then add some orrisroot powder; this is the powdered root of the white flower de luce, a member of the Iris family. You won't need a great deal—start with no more than 1⁄2 ounce (15g). Even a really large mixture will not need more than 2 ounces (55g). This is the fixative and should be no more than a very light snow on the leaves and petals.

Powdered lemon or orange peel (no pith!) can be added too and a little powdered gum bezoin (usually obtainable from a chemist).

Now you have to decide which spice flavor pleases you best; nutmeg or the stronger mace, powdered cloves, coriander, ginger, cinnamon, etc. You can use just a little of all of them if you wish or just one. Add a little at a time, mixing and sniffing until the scent is right. Then add a few drops of flower or leaf oil—rose, geranium, basil, rosemary, sandalwood, cedarwood, lemongrass, verbena, bergamot, etc., which you are sure to find at a chemist's or a health-food shop. You could divide your mixture and use different oil for different batches so that one could have the rich heavy scent of sandalwood and another the clean fresh tang of lemongrass, etc.

When the mixing is done store the mixtures in well-stoppered jars that will not admit light. If you must use glass ones, be sure they are of dark glass. Stir with a wooden spoon every few days for about 6-8 weeks, being careful to stopper the jars well each time.

For the final potting, any pretty jar with a well-fitting lid will do, but you can buy some truly lovely ones that have two lids, the inner one perforated.

When you wish the perfume to be released, take off the pot cover and shake the pot and stand it where a current of air will lift and circulate the fragrance.

I was once selling a house and the agent complimented me on my "ploy." I didn't know what he meant. "That scent of flowers and freshly-roasted coffee," he said. I had just given the potpourri a poke and two coffee beans had become jammed down the side of the hotplate. All unwittingly, it seemed, I had stumbled on a potent inducement to sale. It worked too.

HERB PILLOWS

In the old days when pillows were made of straw, sweet-smelling herbs were added; the idea was to reduce fetid odors and repel germs. There is little need of that these days, but a little herb sachet tucked inside a pillow will certainly give deep pleasure for its scent and possibly act as an inducement to easy sleep.

The herbs can be mixed and put into small muslin or cheesecloth bags and then given pretty covers that can be removed for washing.

Hops and lavender make a nice little bag for insomniacs.

Rose petals and violets; rosemary, mignonette and rose-petals; verbena, marjoram and lavender; woodruff, mint and chamomile, sweet-geranium leaves and rose petals—the list of possibilities is long. You can, if you wish, add a little orrisroot powder and some ground spice— or you can use some of your potpourri.

These bags are also good to tuck inside chair cushions.

It hardly needs saying that the lavender bag gives underclothing and bed linen a beautifully clean fresh scent.

POMANDERS

For instruction as to how to make a pomander—an orange thickly studded with cloves and used in the wardrobe to repel moths—see "Cloves" in the Medicinal Herb section. A pomander can look very pretty and will last for a long time; the orange just gets smaller and smaller and harder and harder. Three pomanders, hung like the three golden balls of the pawnbroker, make a very attractive gift.

ROOM PERFUME

A swab of cotton wool soaked in a fragrant oil and wiped over an electric light bulb will give subtle evening fragrance much less pervasive than that of a joss-stick.

If cooking smells threaten to ruin the atmosphere of a luncheon or dinner party, scatter dried thyme on the warm hotplate of the stove—but don't let it burn.

Cosmetic Herbs

Because of the oils and nutriment contained in their leaves, herbs can be used to make a face wash which is both cleansing and tonic and which is simplicity itself. Just make a pot of herb tea using 3 times the quantity of the fresh leaves or flowers as you would the dried ones, leave until cool, strain and then use.

You can first wash your face, using either soap or lotion, then rinse well. Pour a little of the herb tea into your cupped palms and then hold them against the skin of your face as you lean over the basin; keep repeating the process as the tea drains away. Pat dry. Do not keep the tea for more than 3 days.

FOR A NORMAL SKIN: Cowslip, Fenugreek, Horsetail, Ladies' Bedstraw, Meadowsweet.

FOR A DRY SKIN: Red clover.

FOR AN OILY SKIN: Agrimony, Burdock, Elderflower, Mint, Raspberry, Witch-hazel, Yarrow.

FOR THREADVEINS: Coltsfoot, Marigold, Parsley.

TO FADE FRECKLES: Anise, Dandelion, Fennel.

FOR ACNE: Alfalfa, Burdock, Elecampne, Fumitory, Goosegrass, Hawthorn leaves and berries, Ladies' Mantle, Lovage, Marigold, Nasturtium, Parsley, Sorrel, Tansy, Wild Pansy.

A steam bath made with any of these herbs will open the pores and cleanse the skin. Pour boiling water on the fresh or dried herbs, and lean over the bowl, enclosing head and bowl in a towel.

The tea-bath is treatment at its most rudimentary. A warm compress of the herbs applied to the skin and left for a time will prove of greater help.

Alfalfa and tansy contain substances that can peel away the dead layer of surface skin—they are excellent but should not be used too often.

FOR SUN-DRIED SKIN: Aloe leaf, just cut and the cut side rubbed over the skin. Salad burnet, made into a tea for a face wash.

FOR WRINKLES: Comfrey root. Simmer the root until soft. Strain and pat the water on the skin.

Fennel

Add a little bought witch-hazel lotion to fennel tea and gently pat the liquid on crow's feet and wrinkles.

Witch-hazel

Witch-hazel lotion with a little added lemon juice can be patted on crow's feet but be careful to keep it away from the eyes.

HERBAL MASKS

Face masks can be made using herbal tea and oatmeal, fuller's earth, oil and egg yolks and whites, etc. Once a week is quite enough.

For a dry skin use marshmallow tea made from either the leaves or root with oatmeal, the finer the better or fuller's earth, oil and egg yolk.

For a dry skin, use nettle and yarrow tea to moisten the oatmeal or fuller's earth, together with white of egg and/or brewer's yeast.

Masks should not be made too sloppy. Apply to the face, avoiding the area around the eyes, then lie down and rest while the mask dries. Rinse off with tepid water. Herbal vinegars make good skin toners and astringents but should be diluted before applying to the skin. Elderflowers, lavender flowers, rosemary and yarrow make good cosmetic vinegars.

CREAMS

Simple creams that nourish and soften the skin can be made by adding the herb infusion to oil and honey for short-term keeping and cocoa butter, beeswax any lanolin for larger amounts, which can be stored.

ELDERFLOWER CREAM

1/2 cup oil	4 teaspoonfuls lanolin
freshly picked elderflowers	1 teaspoonful honey

Use just enough flowers to be covered by the oil when pressed down well. Leave to steep overnight. Add lanolin and stir well. Heat very gently and keep at the simmer for at least 20 minutes. Unless you have time to stand over it, use either a double saucepan or stand the pot containing the mixture in the saucepan. Strain and add the liquid honey while still warm enough to make certain the honey will dissolve evenly. Pot when reasonably cool.

Dried elderflowers can be used instead but the fresh flowers are infinitely preferable.

A heavier cream that can be stored is made by using beeswax, but you must include some borax to help the beeswax to break down and give the cream keeping quality.

Use equal quantities beeswax, lanolin and oil and heat gently until the ingredients are smoothly mixed. Add a little borax (no more than a teaspoonful is necessary) to a small but very strong herb tea and heat that gently, stirring to make sure the borax dissolves. Pour the infusion slowly onto the oil mixture and beat as you go. Take it slowly, the cream will only thicken as it cools. Keep beating until you reach a good creamy consistency—too little beating and it will be too runny, too much and the cream will "drag" when applied to the skin. Pot.

ELDERFLOWER OINTMENT

A very simple soothing and smoothing ointment can be made by carefully dissolving a jar of Vaseline over low heat and then adding as many elderflowers as seems feasible and leaving the mixture to simmer very gently for about three-quarters of an hour. Don't let it boil. Sieve, pot, cover when cold. This is good for "housework hands."

HERBAL HAIR TONICS

The simplest possible hair tonic is made with rainwater and herbs. If you simmer rosemary or verbena leaves in rainwater for about 20 minutes and then strain the liquid you have a rinse which can either be used alone or mixed with cider vinegar to give a rinse which will remove the alkaline residue of a bought shampoo which can oft leave the hair dull and without "bounce."

Vinegar has long been known as a splendid hair rinse that keeps the acid balance of the skin of the scalp and so helps to reduce any tendency toward dandruff—herbal vinegars have the added advantage of providing the properties of the herb and, quite often, a delightful scent.

BOCA RATON PUBLIC LIBRARY, FLORIDA

3 3656 0537444 5

The instructions for making herb vinegars can be found in the Culinary Herb section but a simpler way is just to make a strong "tea" of the herb of your choice and then add some cider vinegar. The herbal vinegars themselves should be used diluted—you will only need a tablespoonful to 4 cups (1L) of rinsing water.

Rosemary, chamoline and verbena make scented rinses; burdock, goosegrass, horsetail and nettle, while wonderfully tonic, have little scent but this can be added by a dash of lavender water or by adding some eau-de-Cologne mint leaves to the "brew."

Southernwood has a scent you may feel the need to sweeten and so has sage.

Burdock, goosegrass, horsetail, nettle and southernwood are the best herbs to use when dandruff has become a problem. Rosemary is the best all-round tonic. Sage will help dark hair to keep its color and chamomile will do the same for fair hair.

SHAMPOOS

Lather is not indicative of good cleansing property and is often difficult to remove completely from the hair; a very mild bought shampoo with the addition of herbal tea will not be as "sudsy" but will do a better job and, given a final rinse made with herbal vinegar, the hair will be clean and have more of a natural lift.

See if you can find soapwort root at the herbalist's; it can be bought, ground or grated, I believe, and the tea is said to make an excellent mild shampoo.

For panic situations a good dry shampoo is made by using bought powdered starch with a little orrisroot that has a delicate violet fragrance. The powder should be sprinkled evenly over the hair and gently stroked down to the scalp. After about 15 minutes it should be brushed out with long firm strokes and the powder shaken out of the brush every time.

635.7 Lit
Little, Brenda.
The complete book of herbs
 & spices :